Family Circle
ELM TREE BOOKS

SUCCESSFUL SLIMMING

Dear Readers,

Keeping slim is really just a case of eating sensibly, but, as none of us can be sensible all the time, it is necessary to have the guidelines emphasised, with some recipes for really delicious dishes, so that we don't feel deprived.

The recipes in this book, devised by our cookery editor, Pamela Scott, will help you to reduce weight, then help to keep you slim. We promise that, if you follow our nutritionally-balanced diet, not only will your figure look better, but also your skin and hair – and your health will be better, too.

Here's to a new you!

EDITOR

CONTENTS

WHY SLIM?

Some people might consider that this book is quite unnecessary, that the simplest way to lose weight is to stop eating, so who needs a cookery book if you're not going to cook? You will have to change the way you eat, but you'll see, when you read on, that you can eat satisfying, tasty meals, lose weight and stay slim. Anyway, if you're overweight you probably enjoy eating, so why should you suffer being denied one of the basic necessities of life? You need food to keep you alive and healthy, so, although you'll lose weight if you stop eating, it's dangerous to cut out food altogether.

Overweight

When we speak of overweight, we are referring to an excessive build-up of fat in the body, a condition known as obesity. If you are overweight, it's not because you have a broad bone structure or a heavy build. Some people are overweight because of water retention or for specific medical reasons, but this isn't very common among healthy people.

We need a certain amount of fat to keep us warm: women tend to have a higher proportion of fat in their bodies than men, and are more rounded. Your aim must be to have just enough fat, not too much. Your body is able to convert most of the types of food you eat into fat, so, if you get into the habit of eating more food than your body requires, the daily surplus is converted into fat and stored beneath the skin and around the internal organs. Slowly, this fat accumulates, and so do the pounds and inches. If you don't check your eating habits, your weight can increase alarmingly over the years.

The answer is, first of all, to go on a reducing diet, which means eating less of the energy-giving foods than your body needs, so that you make it use up the fat you have stored. If you stop eating altogether, not only will you feel unwell and quickly lose the will to diet, but the reducing process will be slowed down. You don't have to cut down on the amount of food you eat, just make sure that you cut down on those foods that are most easily converted into fat, if eaten in excess. In other words, you have to start eating a balanced diet that will make your body draw upon its reserves of fat and so make you lose weight.

The next step is to make sure that you maintain the weight loss you have fought so hard to achieve. Fortunately, at this stage, your appetite will be reduced and, if you're honest with yourself, you will know why those extra pounds accumulated in the first place. It's likely that you will have changed your food tastes and will not find it difficult to continue enjoying a balanced diet.

A Balanced Diet

This is the foundation of a good slimming diet and of good health. You eat food, not just because you like it, but in order for your body to obtain certain materials, or nutrients, contained in food, to keep you alive and healthy. In inherently slim people, nature ensures that there is a balance between what your body requires and the amount and type of food they eat. The endocrine glands in the body, particularly the thyroid gland, control the rate at which chemical processes take place, so that people who have a very active thyroid can eat surprisingly large amounts without becoming fat, while those with a less-active thyroid tend to put on weight even though they might eat less. It isn't very fair, but, as no miracle cure has yet been found, this situation will continue and many people will have to keep a special eye on their weight, probably all their lives.

It is very easy not to have a balanced diet, even if you're slim. There are temptations all around us to eat more than we need. You might not put on weight as a result, but your complexion and hair condition could suffer.

Calories are the units in which the heat and energy value of food is measured. However, we don't count Calories in our weight-reducing diet. We think it's better for you to learn straight away which foods will help you to be slim, and to think of food types rather than count Calories. When you eat protein, fat and carbohydrates, you are primarily eating food.

Eventually, instead of the word, 'Calorie', we will use the metric term, 'joule', which has a different value, but still measures the heat and energy of food. The joule serves the same purpose for the slimmer, of course, in that the intake of foods high in joules (which are the same as those high in Calories) must be controlled.

So, you will see, it is useful to know something about the food you eat. It is all made up of a combination of nutrients and, although some foods may contain only one nutrient, most consist of a mixture, each one having a special job to do.

Protein: Needed by the body to provide essential material for growth and the repair of tissue. Children, and pregnant and nursing mothers require more protein, because they are building up new tissue very quickly. Protein is found in both animal and vegetable foods, although animal proteins are, in general, of a higher value. It is important to include meat, fish, cheese, eggs and milk in a slimming diet, as well as vegetables.

Fats and Oils: Provide the body with a concentrated source of heat and energy. If you eat too much of these foods, they can be stored as body fat. As well as in the obvious foods, like butter, lard, cooking fats and oils, margarine, cream and the fat of meat, they are found in a large variety of foods, such as cheese, olives, nuts, mayonnaise, rich sauces and cream desserts.

Carbohydrates: Found in food as either starch or sugar, they also provide your body with a source of heat and energy, though they are not as concentrated a source of Calories as fat. However, because foods containing carbohydrates are relatively inexpensive, a large proportion of a normal diet consists of food such as bread, flour, jam, honey, potatoes, dried and fresh fruit, beans and cereals, to name but a few.

Minerals: Necessary to regulate your body fluids and to ensure that you have strong, healthy bones and teeth. Calcium, iron, phosphorus and sodium are some, but there are many more equally important. Minerals are found in most foods, so, as long as you include a good variety of food in your slimming diet, there is little risk of there being any harmful deficiency. The only possible exception could be iron, so make sure that you eat plenty of green vegetables and liver.

Vitamins: Present in minute quantities in most foods, they are required to regulate the complex chemical processes that keep your body running smoothly. Whereas some vitamins (A,D,E and K) are found only in fatty substances, like margarine and meat fat, others are present only in water-based foods, such as vegetables and fruit.

Unfortunately, there is no 'complete' food, which provides the correct balance of nutrients you need. In any case, you are an individual and your needs differ from those of other people. So, in order to correct the faulty eating habits which caused you to store fat, you have to change the balance of nutrients, so that you lose weight. However, you mustn't cut out any one nutrient completely, because it will probably lead to deficiency of several others.

The Disadvantages of Being Overweight

At one time, being overweight was a sign of affluence, of wealth and good living, but, today, most people in this country enjoy a high standard of living. As a result, more people are overweight, but more people are trying to lose weight, too. In recent years, people have come to realise and to experience the disadvantages of carrying around excess pounds. Some of these are obvious, but many are not: If you've been unable to get into that expensive dress your husband bought you last Christmas, or if you've had to stop running for the bus on your way to work, in order to catch your breath, you'll be aware of two of them. The crunch really comes, though, when you step on the scales.

Most women slim because they want to be fashionable. Nothing is worse for your ego than not being able to buy anything 'off the peg' or having to go to the outsize and often uninspiring and expensive end of the shop. Society today dictates that to be attractive is to be slim, young and active. You can be attractive even if you're overweight, but you'll probably look years older than you actually are and lack a healthy skin or shining, silky hair. And, if there's an opportunity to dance the night away, you'll probably start to tire after the first couple of circuits of the dance floor.

Although the 'cosmetic' reasons for slimming are important in an emotional sense, they are almost insignificant compared with the less-obvious reason that most overweight people are not as healthy as their slim friends. Obesity is now considered to be a major nutritional problem, which can occur at any time of life. Fat people are much more susceptible to a variety of complaints, notably heart diseases, and, on average, one's life expectancy decreases with increasing weight.

Cholesterol

Some overweight people, especially men in middle age, are advised to lose weight and cut down on fat, such as is found in butter, egg yolk, cheese, milk and meat fat. This is because animal fats, termed saturated fats, tend to raise the cholesterol level of the blood and so give overweight people an increased risk of developing coronary disease. This is one of the greatest single killer diseases and it is the fear of this that makes many men go on a slimming or 'health' diet. For this reason, vegetable oils and fats, termed polyunsaturated fats, are healthier for overweight people, because they do not raise the cholesterol level in the blood and are not a danger to health. Doctors advise that other foods, especially offal, should be avoided, too, as they are high in cholesterol.

Overweight in Children

It has been estimated that almost half of the school children in this country are overweight to varying degrees. Medical authorities are extremely concerned about this because fat children are more likely to grow into fat adults, and being overweight can affect their physical and emotional development. Fat children can develop flat feet, knock knees, respiratory difficulties and, in maturity, boys especially often fail to grow to their full height. The plump, bouncing, 'bonny' baby no longer wins prizes at baby shows; the judges now know that the healthy baby is the one that is slim and firm. An overweight baby develops more fat cells than a slim baby and this gives the child a tendency to gain weight and be fat for the rest of his life. No

mother, especially if she is or has been overweight, will want her child to experience the disadvantages and emotional strain being overweight can bring.

If you think that your child is overweight, go to your doctor for advice before you put him on a diet. A child grows very quickly, especially during the early years, and must have the correct nourishment. For a start, though, it's a good idea to cut down on sweets, lollies, cakes and biscuits. Keep a bowl of carrot sticks and celery in the refrigerator for nibbles – the children's teeth will also benefit.

Overweight in Pregnancy

Many women gain more weight than they should during pregnancy, and find it difficult to lose after their baby is born. Usually, a close check is kept on your weight by your doctor, but it is best if you take extra special care of what you eat right from the start. If you are overweight to begin with, you might be advised to lose a few pounds, as you could develop toxaemia, back ache and could experience difficulties during the actual birth. You are, in fact, eating for two, so you need to eat plenty of foods high in protein, vitamins and minerals, but not high in those nutrients, such as fat, sugar and starch, which you'll easily turn into fat, if you eat too much of them.

Slimming Diets

If you have tried to slim before, but haven't been very successful, then you've probably been following one of the many gimmicky 'crash' diets, which have been popular over the past few years. These diets promise to take off a lot of pounds in a very short time. It's very tempting, but then so is a cream bun or a mouth-watering pizza when you've virtually starved yourself or become bored, eating a limited amount and type of food for two or three days.

You can follow these diets for a few days without seriously affecting your health, and probably enjoy the novelty, the first time, of eating bananas and milk, raw steaks and lettuce or oranges and nuts. Any diet will be effective if it provides fewer Calories than you use up each day. You'll lose weight quickly, but, as soon as you start to eat what is your normal diet, the weight you lost (and, perhaps, more) will return even more quickly. You might even have violent feelings of being deprived and ruin everything by raiding the fridge, or having that cream bun.

The ideal diet is one you can keep up because you enjoy it, one that is easy to follow, whether you are at home eating with your family, in a restaurant or pub, or having a packed lunch at the office. It should be substantial and help you to eat in a way that will not only make you slim, but also stop you from ever gaining weight again. But, remember, if you are seriously overweight (you only have to turn to our weight charts on page 9 to discover the awful truth), it's best to consult your doctor and ask his advice before starting to slim.

Eating In

It's a good thing if your slimming diet can be based upon normal family meals. You'll see that our reducing diet fits into a sensible pattern of three substantial meals a day, which all the family can eat. For those in the family who do not need to slim, you can give extra-large portions or supplement their portions with some of the more energy giving foods, such as toast and marmalade at breakfast and bread, potato, thickened sauces, cream and custard at other meals. But, if your family don't cry out for these types of food, don't serve them. It will help to stop your being tempted, as well as giving them a nutritionally-balanced diet. In any case, those in your family who are not trying to lose weight will naturally take snacks while they are away from home.

Every mother likes to have a good store of food in the house. Make sure that most of it fits in with your sensible new eating pattern. If you must have biscuits and cakes in the house, for your own sake put them where you can't see them and stick a notice of warning on the lid that these are not for you, in case the temptation is very strong. Nibbling between meals is the housewife's chief reason for gaining weight. Discreet notices can work wonders, especially if they are placed at eye-level, for when you are walking around and when stooping to take something out of a cupboard. If you are having friends in for a meal, they needn't know that the meal is especially designed to meet your weight-reducing requirements. Just take a look at the menus in our Entertaining section, which begins on page 71, and you'll have no fears about gaining weight next time friends come round for dinner.

You can make up lots of other exciting menus, too, from the other recipes. Your friends might, unknown to you, be on a slimming diet, too, and really appreciate a less-rich, but tasty and filling, meal. You can serve some other accompaniments, such as roast potatoes or fresh cream, which your guests might like, but you won't take, of course.

Serve alcoholic drinks for guests and wine with the meal, if you wish, but for slimmers, there is an entire section of drinks recipes starting on page 83.

Eating Out

Eating is very much a social occasion and most of us like to eat out at a restaurant. If you are at a friend's home, then it's rather difficult to refuse what is served to you, so eat it, don't make a fuss, and, above all, enjoy it. For a couple of days afterwards, eat the least fattening of foods, plenty of salad and cottage cheese and eggs, to compensate. If you decide to eat before going out, eat plenty of these 'light' foods, so that you are not ravenous by the time you get to the restaurant and so eat everything you can, regardless of your diet.

When you go to a restaurant, try to choose one you know has something on the menu that you can eat safely. If you cannot choose where you eat, and find that everything on the menu is fried, coated in rich sauces or served with hearty helpings of starchy and sweet foods, you have to be rather more careful and selective. For a starter, order a clear soup (no roll), fruit or a light hors d'oeuvre. Eat the meat or fish and vegetables or salad, but forget the sauce on your main course. And, when you give your order, ask for your meal to be served without chips, roast potatoes or rice, so that you're not tempted.

Often, you can have fresh fruit for a dessert, but, if the fruit cocktail comes out of a can, eat the fruit, but not the syrup. If there isn't a dessert you feel safe in choosing, perhaps you can revert to the starters and have melon or grapefruit. Otherwise, avoid 'gooey' desserts, gâteaux and cream. Better still, exclaim how full you are after the main course and have two coffees instead. Avoid alcohol, if you can – it's packed full of Calories. There are plenty of low Calorie carbonated drinks available in bars and restaurants, but, if you can't order these, soda water with plenty of ice and slices of lemon or orange is very refreshing. You'll have the satisfaction of having a sociable glass in your hand, knowing that it won't put on pounds. Of course, you can drink as much tea and coffee as you want, sweetened with one of the many sugar substitutes available, if you like.

Those not aiming to lose weight, but who are being careful not to put on any pounds, should choose alcoholic drinks which are lowest in Calories. Choose light, dry table wines, like Muscadet, Pouilly Fuissé, Soave or Bernkastler. If your taste is for red wine, the wines known as claret, from the Bordeaux region of France, are the lowest in Calories – Medoc and St. Emilion are such wines. Otherwise, choose a small measure of gin or whisky, topped up with soda water or water and ice, and drink it slowly to make it last a long time.

Packed Lunches

You'll see on the reducing diet that we've catered for those of you who take a packed lunch to work. Often, it's difficult to think of varied and interesting menus, but with a little forethought, you can make up appetising and filling lunch boxes for yourself, your husband and children. Different sorts of salads will keep well in plastic boxes. Coleslaw can be mixed with a little low Calorie vinegar and oil dressing, which is very like mayonnaise, and packed the night before. But mixed salads and green salads are best tossed in a little wine vinegar and seasoning, or French dressing just before serving; a small bottle of dressing could be packed with the lunch. Fresh fruit salad also keeps well in plastic containers overnight. Use a liquid sweetener in place of sugar and toss the fruit in a little lemon juice, to prevent browning.

There are lots of wrappings which are ideal for carrying food to work, such as foil or self-clinging plastic wrap. You can cook a chicken portion in a double layer of foil and simply carry the parcel to work the following day. Cottage-cheese cartons, with lids, and other plastic containers are ideal for small quantities of food.

If your husband is on a diet, but likes to have a 'liquid lunch' in a pub with his friends, he might find it a little difficult, especially if his friends aren't too sympathetic towards his efforts. Encourage him to stand firm and drink low Calorie drinks, or to drink just one glass of light beer, instead of three or four of brown ale or a heavy stout. Alternatively, he might prefer to have spirits topped with water, low Calorie tonic or soda water and ice. Pack him a slimmer's lunch box, so that he doesn't have to eat greasy sausages, scotch eggs and sandwiches, the usual type of food served in pubs. Or encourage him to eat only one meat sandwich and pop a piece of fruit in his working case or coat pocket to eat as well. It has been found that men make the most resolute slimmers, usually because they are slimming for their good health, often associated with being able to obtain a good insurance. The insurance companies consider overweight people to be a high risk. So, it's up to you, his wife or girlfriend, to help him all you can, by not feeding him fattening food. No doubt, his achievements will help you to keep to your diet, too.

Before You Start

Read all the different sections carefully, so you know exactly how to go about changing your eating habits, and your size. As you lose weight, it might be a good idea to increase the amount of exercise you take, to help tone up your muscles, so that you'll be nice and firm when you're slim. Walking will help, even if only to the shops, instead of taking a short bus ride or going by car. You'll find the exercises given at the back of this book very helpful, if you fit a few into your daily routine.

You will notice that both imperial and metric quantities are given in the reducing diet and the recipes. This is to help you adjust to the metric system of measurement, which will be widely used quite soon in this country. Although the equivalent imperial and metric weights and liquid measures may vary slightly, allowances have been made for this in the recipes – and, in the diet, it is the actual balance of nutrients which is important. The differences are so small as to be virtually insignificant.
✱ The recipes marked with a star are the ones to follow for a weight-reducing diet.

YOUR IDEAL WEIGHT

The charts below give your ideal weight, without shoes and dressed in light, indoor clothing. However, remember that you are an individual, and that your weight could be just over 2kg (up to 5 pounds) above or below the figures given. Be honest with yourself about your frame size and don't pretend that you have a large frame, when really you are quite small! In order to record an accurate weight loss:

1. Weigh yourself only once each week—your weight fluctuates daily, so the weight you've lost over a week is an accurate average.

2. Weigh yourself at the same time of day—you will be heavier at bed time than first thing in the morning. Don't fool yourself by getting weighed early in the morning, if you weighed yourself in the evening the week before. There could be several vital pounds' difference.

3. Wear the same or similar weight clothing each time you get on to the scales.

4. Use the same weighing scales every week, so that your weight loss is accurate, even if the scales themselves have a slight error.

5. Stand on the scales without moving or touching anything with your hands. You may weigh lighter, if you do, but the pounds will still be there!

6. Write down your starting weight, your target weight and the number of pounds or kilograms you have to lose. If you do gain weight for some reason (for women, this could be just before your period starts), write that down, too, as this will help you keep to your diet in the week to come.

IDEAL WEIGHT CHART FOR MEN

HEIGHT				SMALL FRAME			MEDIUM FRAME			LARGE FRAME		
ft	in	m	cm	st	lb	kg	st	lb	kg	st	lb	kg
5	1	1	56	8	2	51.8	8	9	55	9	4	59.1
5	2	1	58	8	6	53.6	8	13	56.8	9	8	60.9
5	3	1	61	8	9	55	9	1	57.7	9	11	62.3
5	4	1	63	8	11	55.9	9	5	59.5	10	0	63.6
5	5	1	66	9	0	57.3	9	8	60.9	10	4	65.4
5	6	1	68	9	4	59.1	9	11	62.3	10	9	67.7
5	7	1	71	9	8	60.9	10	3	65	10	13	69.5
5	8	1	73	9	12	62.7	10	7	66.8	11	4	71.8
5	9	1	76	10	3	65	10	11	68.6	11	7	73.2
5	10	1	78	10	7	66.8	11	0	70	11	13	75.9
5	11	1	81	10	11	68.6	11	4	71.8	12	3	77.7
6	0	1	84	11	0	70	11	10	74.5	12	9	80.4
6	1	1	86	11	3	71.4	12	0	76.4	12	13	82.3
6	2	1	89	11	7	73.2	12	6	79.1	13	4	84.5
6	3	1	91	11	11	75	12	10	80.9	13	8	86.4

IDEAL WEIGHT CHART FOR WOMEN

HEIGHT				SMALL FRAME			MEDIUM FRAME			LARGE FRAME		
ft	in	m	cm	st	lb	kg	st	lb	kg	st	lb	kg
4	8	1	42	6	9	42.3	7	1	45	7	11	49.5
4	9	1	44	6	11	43.2	7	3	45.9	8	0	50.9
4	10	1	47	7	0	44.5	7	7	47.7	8	3	52.2
4	11	1	50	7	3	45.9	7	9	48.6	8	6	53.6
5	0	1	52	7	5	46.8	7	11	49.5	8	9	55
5	1	1	56	7	9	48.6	8	0	50.9	8	12	56.4
5	2	1	58	7	12	50	8	4	52.7	9	1	57.7
5	3	1	61	8	0	50.9	8	9	55	9	5	59.5
5	4	1	63	8	4	52.7	8	13	56.8	9	9	61.3
5	5	1	66	8	8	54.6	9	3	58.6	9	13	63.1
5	6	1	68	8	12	56.4	9	7	60.5	10	3	65
5	7	1	71	9	3	58.6	9	11	62.3	10	6	66.3
5	8	1	73	9	7	60.5	10	1	64.1	10	11	68.5
5	9	1	76	9	10	61.7	10	5	65.9	11	2	70.8
5	10	1	78	9	13	63.1	10	9	67.7	11	6	72.6

FOOD GUIDE

EAT MODERATE PORTIONS OF THE FOLLOWING:

MEAT, FISH, ETC
Fresh or canned mackerel
Game
Lean meat
Poultry
Rabbit
Shellfish (fresh, frozen or canned)
Smoked cod and haddock
Tuna and salmon (canned)
White fish

VEGETABLES
Bean sprouts
Brussels sprouts
Cabbage
Cauliflower
Courgettes
Green and red peppers
Green beans
Kale
Leaf spinach
Leeks
Marrow
Mushrooms
Onions
Sauerkraut
Spring greens
Tomatoes
Unsweetened pickled vegetables

SALAD
Celery
Chicory
Chives
Cucumber
Endive
Lettuce
Mustard and cress
Parsley
Radishes
Tomatoes
Watercress

DAIRY FOODS
Cheese: cottage, curd or Edam
Eggs
Low-fat or fat-free natural yoghourt

FRESH FRUIT
Apples
Apricots
Grapefruit
Lemons
Melon
Oranges
Peaches
Pineapple
Plums
Raspberries
Strawberries

DRINKS
Fruit juices (fresh or unsweetened)
Low Calorie carbonated drinks
Low Calorie concentrated fruit
    drinks
Soda water
Tea and coffee, sweetened with liquid
    sweetener (milk from allowance)
Tomato juice
Vegetable juices
Water

MISCELLANEOUS
Beef extract
Dried vegetable flakes
Garlic
Herbs (fresh or dried)
Natural essences
Natural flavourings
Seasonings
Spices
Stock cubes
Sugar substitute (liquid or tablets)
Worcester sauce
Yeast extract
(See also daily allowance)

INCLUDE OCCASIONALLY:

Lean pork, bacon, ham, hard
(Cheddar-type) cheese, carrots, peas,
turnips, swedes, beetroot, grapes,
bananas, cherries.

AVOID THE FOLLOWING:

Avocado pears
Beer
Biscuits
Bread (see daily allowance)
Buns
Butter and margarine (see daily
    allowance)
Cakes
Canned fruit
Chipped potatoes
Chocolate
Chutneys
Cocoa
Cream
Cream cheese
Custard powder
Dried fruit
Duck
Fat and fatty meats
Flour or cornflour
Ice cream
Jam and honey
Lager beer
Lemon curd
Luncheon meat
Marmalade
Mayonnaise and salad cream
Mincemeat
Mousses
Nuts
Oily fish
Pasta
Pastry
Potatoes
Puddings
Rice
Sausages
Spirits
Sugar
Sweet corn
Sweet sauces and sweetened pickles
Sweet wines and cider
Sweets
Thickened soups, gravies and
    sauces (with flour or cornflour)

DAILY ALLOWANCES

*Try to include in your daily eating pattern your
choice from each of the following four sections:*

FAT:
15g (½oz) margarine or butter
or 25g (1oz) low-fat spread
or 2 level tablespoons low Calorie vinegar and oil
  dressing
or 1 x 15ml spoon (1 tablespoon) vegetable oil (not
  to be used for frying)

MILK:
50g (2oz) dried skimmed milk (reconstituted as
  desired)
or 250ml (½ pint) whole milk

BREAD:
2 slices starch-reduced bread (men, 3 slices)
or 3 crispbreads (men, 4 crispbreads)
or 2 starch-reduced rolls (men, 3 rolls)
or once or twice each week, exchange 1 slice of
  starch-reduced bread, 2 crispbreads or 1 starch-
  reduced roll for 1 medium-sized boiled potato or
  jacket-baked potato, or 4 x 15ml spoons (2
  rounded tablespoons) boiled rice

FRUIT:
2 or 3 portions fresh fruit, or 150ml (5 fluid oz)
portions of unsweetened fruit juice

DAILY MEAL PATTERN

*Try to eat three substantial meals a day. Start
with a nourishing breakfast, as suggested
below, and eat two other satisfying meals during
the day. Include the items chosen from the four
Daily Allowance sections, as desired.*

ON WAKING
Tea or coffee, if desired, using milk from allowance and liquid sweetener

BREAKFAST
1 glass fruit juice (150ml, 5 fluid oz)
or half a grapefruit (no sugar)
or 1 portion fresh fruit
  1 egg (boiled, poached or scrambled without fat)
or 25g (1oz) hard cheese
or 50g (2oz) cottage cheese
or 1 rasher lean, grilled bacon
or 1 (150ml, 5 fluid oz) carton fat-free or low-fat
  natural yoghourt
or occasionally, 1 kipper, or small bowl of starch-
  reduced cornflakes (no sugar; use milk from
  allowance)
  bread and fat from allowance
  tea or coffee

MID-MORNING
Tea, coffee, yeast extract or stock-cube drink
bread and fat from allowance, if desired

MAIN COURSE DISHES
Soup, if desired; moderate portion meat, fish,
  poultry or offal (see starred recipes)
or 2 eggs
or 50g (2oz) hard cheese
or 100g (4oz) cottage cheese
  moderate portion of vegetables
  salad, as desired
  fresh fruit, unsweetened fruit juice or a dessert,
  if desired (see starred recipes)
  bread and fat from allowance
  tea or coffee

AFTERNOON
Tea or coffee
bread, fruit or dessert, if not eaten at lunch

EVENING OR BED-TIME
Tea or coffee
bread, fruit or dessert, if not eaten during the day

11

MENU PLAN FOR WEIGHT REDUCING DIET

WEEK ONE	SUNDAY	MONDAY	TUESDAY	WEDNESDAY	THURSDAY	FRIDAY	SATURDAY
BREAKFAST	Fruit juice Grilled bacon 1 slice toast Tea or coffee	1 orange Cheese 1 slice toast Tea or coffee	Half a grape-fruit Scrambled egg 1 crispbread Tea or coffee	Fruit juice Grilled bacon 1 starch-reduced roll Tea or coffee	1 small banana Yoghourt Tea or coffee	Large glass tomato juice 1 kipper or cottage cheese 1 slice toast Tea or coffee	Half a grape-fruit Poached egg 1 slice toast Tea or coffee
MID-MORNING	Coffee	*Lemon Tea	Coffee	Chicken stock cube drink	Coffee 1 crispbread	Tea	Coffee
LUNCH	*Clear Vegetable Soup *Celery-stuffed Roast Lamb Carrots Brussels sprouts *Sugar-free Mint Sauce *Melon Bowl Fruit Salad	Cold, sliced lamb Green beans Tomato salad 1 crispbread 2 fresh plums or 1 apple	*Fish Dolmas with Mushrooms Salad, if desired 1 slice bread *Fruit-flavour Jelly (orange)	25g (1oz) Edam cheese 50g (2oz) cottage cheese Mixed salad 2 crispbreads with yeast extract	*Baked Eggs with Ham 1 starch-reduced roll Mixed salad *Apple Fool	*Cauliflower Onion Soup *Mushroom and Bacon Toasts 1 pear	Tongue Mixed salad 1 crispbread 1 orange
PACKED LUNCH		1 lamb sandwich 2 tomatoes Celery sticks 2 fresh plums or 1 apple	1 tuna sandwich or 1 roast chicken portion and 2 crispbreads 2 tomatoes Cucumber	1 Edam cheese sandwich 50g (2oz) cottage cheese Carrot sticks Lettuce	2 boiled eggs 1 starch-reduced roll Radishes Celery sticks 1 apple	*Cauliflower Onion Soup or beef stock cube drink 1 bacon sand-wich 25g (1oz) Blue cheese 1 tomato	
MID-AFTERNOON	*Iced Tea	Tea	Tea 1 peach or orange	Tea 1 apple	*Lemon Tea	Tea 1 pear	Coffee
DINNER OR HIGH TEA	Salmon or tuna Mixed salad 2 crispbreads *Orange Dream Cups (no wafers)	*Mustard Cod Grill Carrots Broccoli or cauliflower Small salad 1 peach	*Ox Liver Casserole *Parsleyed Turnips *Quick Apple Crumble	*Minted Orange and Grapefruit *Braised Beef with Tomatoes Cabbage or spring greens	*Mackerel Bake Peas Small salad 1 orange	*Glazed Grilled Chicken Carrots Mixed salad Stewed Rhubarb with *Vanilla Ice or *Quick 'Cream'	*Savoury Leeks Grilled Tomato 1 slice toast Small salad *Fruit-flavour Jelly (lime) Fresh sliced pears
BED TIME	Tea or coffee	Stock cube drink 1 crispbread	Tea or coffee	*Hot Savoury Drink	Tea or coffee	Tea or coffee	*Hot Savoury Drink

*Look for these dishes in the following recipe sections.

USING THE MENU PLAN

THIS menu plan gives a suggested weight-reducing eating pattern for 14 consecutive days. Each day consists of three meals, which will fit in with family eating, and includes a packed lunch for each weekday, for those who are away from home at some meal times.

The plan for each day shows how the Daily Meal Pattern can be organised to include a wide variety of the permitted foods, yet be substantial enough to stop you yearning for those forbidden, fattening foods. Follow the menus, as given, or select a day's meals or recipes from the menu plan and make up menus of your own. Make sure you include a good variety of foods, and that they fit in with your daily eating pattern.

There are a large number of other recipes in the recipe sections not included on the suggested menu plans. Those that are starred can be used in the weight-reducing diet. When you have lost all your excess weight, try some of the recipes that are not starred, as these are designed to help you maintain your weight, and permit you to eat some of the foods you have had to avoid while on the weight-reducing diet.

Start the day with a substantial breakfast, so you won't be tempted to nibble early in the day. If you are a 'nibbler', prepare a bowl of raw vegetables, such as

WEEK TWO	SUNDAY	MONDAY	TUESDAY	WEDNESDAY	THURSDAY	FRIDAY	SATURDAY
BREAKFAST	Stewed apple Yoghourt Tea or coffee	Half a grape-fruit Boiled egg 1 slice toast Tea or coffee	1 orange Cornflakes Tea or coffee	Fruit juice Cottage cheese 1 slice toast Tea or coffee	Half a grape-fruit Grilled bacon 1 slice toast Tea or coffee	Fruit juice Cheese 1 crispbread Tea or coffee	1 orange Scrambled egg 1 slice toast Tea or coffee
MID-MORNING	Coffee	Beef stock cube drink	*Lemon Tea	Coffee	*Hot Savoury Drink	Coffee	*Lemon Tea
LUNCH	Tomato juice Roast chicken 1 boiled potato Baked tomato Green beans *Strawberry and Orange Cups	Chicken or cottage cheese Mixed salad 2 crispbreads with yeast extract	1 slice lean ham 50g(2oz) cottage cheese *Picuto Salad Lettuce 1 slice bread	*Shrimp Salad 2 slices bread	*Egg and Spinach Grill 2 crispbreads Small portion grapes or 1 apple	*Grilled Mackerel Grilled tomato Boiled celery Fresh fruit	*Creamy Watercress Soup Grilled steak Mushrooms Broccoli
PACKED LUNCH		Cottage cheese Cos lettuce Celery sticks Tomato 2 crispbreads with yeast extract	1 ham sandwich 50g(2oz) cottage cheese 2 tomatoes 1 pear	*Shrimp Salad 2 tomato sandwiches	1 egg sandwich 25g(1oz) Edam cheese Carrot sticks Small portion grapes or 1 apple	*Potted Mackerel 2 crispbreads Celery sticks 1 tomato Fresh fruit	
MID-AFTERNOON	*Lime and Ginger Cooler	Tea 1 apple or peach	Tea	Coffee 1 apple	*Lemon Tea	Tea	*Frappé 1 apple or orange
DINNER OR HIGH TEA	Ham and cheese salad Grated carrot 1 crispbread 2 rings pine-apple (canned in natural juice) *Whisked Dessert Topping or *Quick 'Cream'	*Liver in Tomato Sauce Cauliflower Peas Small salad 1 orange	Grilled Haddock Mushrooms Tomato Small salad Fruit juice or *Valencia Fruit Salad	*Creamy Pea Soup *Kidney Casserole Brussels sprouts Small salad 1 tangerine or orange	Poached smoked cod Green beans Tomato salad Fruit juice or 2 apricots	*Lamb Chops Provence 1 crispbread Spring onion and cucumber salad *Quick 'Bake' Apple *Quick 'Cream'	Fruit juice *Foil-baked Whiting Cabbage Small cube Edam cheese 1 crispbread
BED TIME	Tea or coffee 1 crispbread	*Vanilla Milk Punch	*Hot Savoury Drink	Tea or coffee	*Hot Tomato Cocktail	Tea or coffee	Tea or coffee 1 apple or pear

*Look for these dishes in the following recipe sections.

celery sticks, shredded cabbage, radishes, carrots and cucumber, and make up some of the tasty soups for between-meal snacks. If you go out to work, these can be carried in a plastic container or vacuum flask, which will fit into a shopping bag or desk drawer.

At mid-morning, a drink and a snack taken from your Daily Allowance will stave off any hunger pangs you may have until lunch time. But, if you've eaten a breakfast as described in our eating pattern, you shouldn't feel hungry at all. You'll find that your appetite will diminish as you become accustomed to eating regular and satisfying meals.

A light, mid-day meal or packed lunch is given in the menu plan, but, if you prefer a heavier cooked meal, choose one of the meals described for the evening, and eat the light meal at night as a high tea. The packed lunches can also be used as picnic meals, and the ingredients are almost the same as those used in the mid-day meal that is eaten at home. The sandwiches all use just one slice of starch-reduced bread, so pack it with filling, according to the amounts suggested in the Daily Meal Pattern. A drink and, perhaps, a snack taken during the afternoon will help you to get through the afternoon without cheating (though you would only be cheating yourself). You could choose bread, fruit or a dessert from your Daily Allowance, if you wish, as your snack, if any of these are not eaten at lunch time, or vegetables from your 'nibble' bowl. In the evening, tuck into any food remaining from your Daily Allowance, such as milk and fruit. It's a good idea to save something to look forward to after the last meal of the day. Where food items suggested on the menu plan are not available or are out of season, choose something similar from the permitted foods list as a substitute.

COOKING TIPS

SIMPLE methods of cooking usually produce food that is lower in Calories. They also help to retain the natural flavours, so often lost when meals are overloaded with fat, cream, rich sauces and sugar. When on our reducing diet, do not fry any food in fat—dry-fry, using a non-stick frying pan instead, and grill, poach and steam food. Wrap meat, fish and poultry in foil before roasting, so that they cook in their own juices and retain the maximum flavour. Remove the skin from poultry and any visible fat from meat before cooking, where possible.

Experiment with herbs, seasonings and other flavourings, as indicated in our permitted-food guide, to make every meal as exciting as possible, so you don't become bored with slimming. The recipes for delicious dishes included in our 14-day weight-reducing menu plan will help you to achieve this, and give you ideas for other recipes, which you'll find yourself making up as you go along.

Cook vegetables until they are just tender, yet still a little crisp. Over-cooked vegetables lose some of the vital nutrients and are not very appetising.

Try cooking vegetables with a stock cube, various herbs and flavourings, and save the cooking liquid as a base for soups. The liquid saved from cooking peas, green beans, celery and onions is especially delicious.

Do not thicken sauces, gravies or soups with flour or cornflour. Where possible, thicken with an egg or remove the slimmer's portion before thickening the remainder in the normal way for the rest of the family. Do not use sugar to sweeten any food. There are many artificial sweeteners available in both liquid and tablet form. Don't eat anything containing sorbitol, as this is a sweetener for diabetics, not slimmers, and is fattening.

You'll find these cooking tips invaluable on the reducing diet. You will probably continue to follow them, even when you've lost all your excess weight and can gradually start to include items, such as thickened sauces and a few fried foods, if you wish. The recipes that are starred on our 14-day menu plan are given in the following recipe sections, together with other starred recipes, which, although not included in the menu plan, can be introduced as alternatives to those suggested.

STARTERS AND LIGHT MAIN MEALS

Cauliflower Onion Soup ✱

(pictured opposite and on front cover)

For 4 portions:

IMPERIAL	METRIC
½lb cauliflower (about half a medium-sized one)	¼kg cauliflower (about half a medium-sized one)
2 medium-sized onions	2 medium-sized onions
1 teaspoon oil	1 x 5ml spoon oil
1 chicken stock cube	1 chicken stock cube
Salt and pepper	Salt and pepper
¼ level teaspoon grated nutmeg	½ x 2.5ml spoon grated nutmeg
3 rounded tablespoons dried skimmed milk	6 x 15ml spoons dried skimmed milk
Chopped parsley	Chopped parsley

1. Wash cauliflower; cut into small sprigs and chop stalk. Peel and finely chop onions.
2. Place oil in a large saucepan, add onion and cook for 2 to 3 minutes. Stir in 250ml (½ pint) water, stock cube 1 x 2.5ml spoon (½ level teaspoon) salt, a shake of pepper and nutmeg. Bring to boil, stirring; add cauliflower, cover and cook for 20 to 25 minutes, until cauliflower is tender.
3. Sieve soup, or liquidise in an electric blender. Rinse saucepan; return soup to pan, stirring.
4. Place skimmed milk in a measuring jug and make up to 400ml (¾ pint) with water; add to saucepan.
5. Bring slowly to boil. Taste and add more salt and pepper, if necessary. Serve immediately, sprinkled with chopped parsley.

Minted Orange and Grapefruit ✱

For 4 portions:

IMPERIAL	METRIC
2 grapefruit	2 grapefruit
1 large orange	1 large orange
2 rounded teaspoons chopped mint	4 x 5ml spoons chopped mint
Small sprigs of mint	Small springs of mint

1. Cut each grapefruit in half, horizontally; cut around fruit segments with a sharp, pointed knife. Place fruit in a basin; reserve grapefruit shells. Remove pith from fruit with scissors.
2. Using a sharp or serrated knife, cut peel from orange, including white pith; hold orange over basin, to catch juice; cut out segments of orange. Place segments in basin with grapefruit. Add chopped mint and mix well. Leave in a cool place for at least 1 hour for flavours to blend.
3. Just before serving, pile fruit into grapefruit shells and decorate each with a small sprig of mint.

Mushroom and Bacon Toasts ✱

(pictured opposite)

For 4 portions:

IMPERIAL	METRIC
½lb button mushrooms	¼kg button mushrooms
4 rashers back bacon	4 rashers back bacon
4 slices starch-reduced bread	4 slices starch-reduced bread
1 tablespoon lemon juice	1 x 15ml spoon lemon juice
1 level teaspoon chopped parsley	1 x 5ml spoon chopped parsley
½ level teaspoon salt	1 x 2.5ml spoon salt
Pepper	Pepper
1oz low-fat spread	25g low-fat spread
Watercress	Watercress
2 large tomatoes	2 large tomatoes

1. Wash mushrooms. Trim and chop stalks; cut mushrooms in halves.
2. Remove rind and fat from bacon and reserve. Press rashers flat with the back of a knife. Cut in halves; roll up each rasher loosely.
3. Remove grill pan and prepare a hot grill. Place bacon rolls and bread on grill rack and return pan to grill. Toast bread on both sides; turn bacon once during cooking. Keep warm.
4. Place rind and fat from bacon into a large saucepan. Heat gently until fat begins to flow and bottom of pan is thinly coated with bacon fat. Discard fat and rind.
5. Add lemon juice, mushrooms, parsley, salt and a shake of pepper to pan. Cover and cook gently for 3 to 4 minutes, shaking pan occasionally. Remove mushrooms and keep warm. Quickly boil juices in pan until reduced to about 1 tablespoonful. Add mushrooms and quickly reheat for 1 minute.
6. Spread toast with low-fat spread. Pile mushrooms on toast and top with bacon rolls. Spoon juices from pan over mushrooms. Serve immediately, with watercress and tomato wedges.

CAULIFLOWER ONION SOUP
MUSHROOM AND BACON
TOASTS

Crisp Salad Starter *

For 4 portions:

IMPERIAL	METRIC
2in piece of cucumber	5cm piece of cucumber
1 stick of celery	1 stick of celery
1 large tomato	1 large tomato
2 oz wedge white cabbage	50g wedge white cabbage
1 tablespoon wine vinegar	1 x 15ml spoon wine vinegar
½ level teaspoon salt	1 x 2.5ml spoon salt
Black pepper	Black pepper
8 sprigs watercress	8 sprigs watercress

1. Cut cucumber into small dice; wash celery and cut into thin slices; chop tomato.

2. Finely shred cabbage. Place wine vinegar, salt and a little black pepper in a serving bowl. Add prepared vegetables and toss lightly.

3. Garnish with sprigs of watercress and serve as a starter with low-calorie vinegar and oil dressing, or as a side salad on a bed of lettuce.

NOTE: Any combination of salad vegetables can be used, such as red or green pepper, finely chopped onion, pickled cauliflower, grated or diced carrot, cooked peas or sliced mushrooms.

Mushroom Soup *

For 4 portions:

IMPERIAL	METRIC
1 small onion	1 small onion
½ lb button mushrooms	¼ kg button mushrooms
1 chicken stock cube	1 chicken stock cube
¼ level teaspoon mixed dried herbs	½ x 2.5ml spoon mixed dried herbs
2 level teaspoons chopped parsley	1 x 10ml spoon chopped parsley
1oz dried skimmed milk	25g dried skimmed milk
Salt and pepper	Salt and pepper

1. Peel and finely chop onion. Wash mushrooms; reserve 6 and finely chop remainder.

2. Place onion, chopped mushrooms, stock cube, herbs, 1 level teaspoon chopped parsley and ½ litre (1 pint) water in a medium-sized saucepan. Bring to boil; reduce heat, cover and simmer for 20 minutes, stirring occasionally. Leave to cool slightly.

3. Place dried skimmed milk in a liquidiser goblet; add contents of pan and run machine until mixture is well blended. Rinse saucepan; return soup to saucepan.

4. Finely slice reserved mushrooms. Add to saucepan and bring to boil, stirring. Cook for 2 minutes, then remove from heat. Taste and season with salt and pepper. Serve garnished with remaining chopped parsley.

Red Pepper Soup *

For 4 to 6 portions:

IMPERIAL	METRIC
1 small cauliflower	1 small cauliflower
1 medium-sized red pepper	1 medium-sized red pepper
1 small onion	1 small onion
2 chicken stock cubes	2 chicken stock cubes
½ level teaspoon mustard	1 x 2.5ml spoon mustard
Salt and pepper	Salt and pepper

1. Wash cauliflower; cut into small springs, chop stalk and any tender leaves. Place in a large saucepan. Cut pepper in half, lengthwise; discard seeds, core and white pith. Cut pepper into small dice. Peel and chop onion.

2. Place onion, stock cubes, mustard and half the diced red pepper in saucepan. Add 1 litre (1¾ pints) water. Bring to boil, stirring; cover and simmer for 25 to 30 minutes, until cauliflower is tender.

3. Place contents of pan in a liquidiser goblet and run machine until mixture is well blended. (Do not over-fill liquidiser goblet; divide soup into 2 or more batches.) Rinse saucepan; return soup to saucepan.

4. Add remaining diced red pepper to saucepan. Bring to boil, stirring. Remove from heat; taste and season with salt and pepper. Serve hot.

Creamy Watercress Soup *

For 4 portions:

IMPERIAL	METRIC
1 medium-sized onion	1 medium-sized onion
1 large bunch watercress	1 large bunch watercress
2 chicken stock cubes	2 chicken stock cubes
1 piece mace	1 piece mace
¼ level teaspoon dried basil	½ x 2.5ml spoon dried basil
2 rounded tablespoons dried skimmed milk	4 x 15ml spoon dried skimmed milk
Salt and black pepper	Salt and black pepper

1. Peel and finely chop onion.

2. Wash watercress and discard any brown leaves; reserve several springs for garnish and cut remainder into pieces. Place onion, watercress, stock cubes, mace and basil in a medium-sized saucepan. Add ¾ litre (1½ pints) water. Bring to boil, cover and simmer for 20 minutes, stirring occasionally. Leave to cool slightly.

3. Place contents of pan in a liquidiser goblet. Add dried skimmed milk and run machine until the mixture is well blended.

4. Rinse saucepan. Return soup to saucepan and reheat gently. Taste and season with salt and black pepper. Serve hot, garnished with reserved springs of watercress.

Spinach Soup *

For 4 portions:

IMPERIAL	METRIC
1 chicken stock cube	1 chicken stock cube
1 small (4½oz) carton frozen chopped spinach	1 small (127g) carton frozen chopped spinach
1 egg	1 egg

1. Place ½ litre (1 pint) water, stock cube and frozen spinach in a saucepan. Bring to boil, cover and simmer for 5 minutes.
2. Beat egg in a basin or jug. Pour a little soup on to egg, mix with a wooden spoon and return to saucepan. Stir for a few minutes until slightly thickened (do not boil). Serve immediately.

Savoury Stuffed Tomatoes

For 4 portions:

IMPERIAL	METRIC
2 rashers back bacon	2 rashers back bacon
4 large tomatoes	4 large tomatoes
1oz Edam cheese	25g Edam cheese
4oz cottage cheese	100g cottage cheese
A few seedless raisins (optional)	A few seedless raisins (optional)
1 level teaspoon chopped parsley	1 x 5ml spoon chopped parsley
¼ level teaspoon salt	½ x 2.5ml spoon salt
Black pepper	Black pepper

GARNISH	GARNISH
2 cos lettuce leaves	2 cos lettuce leaves
Parsley	Parsley
Sliced celery	Sliced celery

1. Remove rind and bone from bacon and cut bacon into small pieces. Fry until crisp and drain well on kitchen paper; leave to cool.
2. Cut off the top of each tomato and reserve for 'lids'. Scoop out inside with a teaspoon and place in a sieve over a basin. Leave to drain thoroughly; discard juice and any hard core; finely chop pulp.
3. Grate Edam cheese finely. Place bacon, tomato pulp, cheeses, raisins, if used, parsley, salt and a shake of pepper in a basin. Mix together well.
4. Press mixture into tomato shells and top each with a lid.
5. Place lettuce leaves together on an oblong serving plate, to form a canoe shape. Place stuffed tomatoes in a line on lettuce leaves and place a sprig of parsley between each tomato. Arrange sliced celery on plate around lettuce leaves. Serve with toasted starch-reduced bread, rolls or crispbread and low-fat spread, if desired.
NOTE: For a main course, double the quantities and serve 2 tomatoes per portion.

Fluffy Cottage Eggs *

For 4 portions:

IMPERIAL	METRIC
4 eggs	4 eggs
4oz cooked ham	100g cooked ham
8oz cottage cheese	200g cottage cheese
½ level teaspoon salt	1 x 2.5ml spoon salt
Black pepper	Black pepper
1 large (12oz) packet frozen sliced green beans	1 large (339g) packet frozen sliced green beans

1. Prepare a moderate oven (190 deg C, 375 deg F, Gas Mark 5). Lightly grease 4 (250ml, ½ pint) individual ovenproof dishes.
2. Separate eggs; place whites in a clean, grease-free bowl and yolks in a separate bowl. Chop ham.
3. Add cheese, ham, salt and a shake of pepper to yolks and beat well.
4. Whisk egg whites until stiff, but not dry. Fold into egg, cheese and ham mixture, using a metal spoon. Divide mixture between the 4 dishes.
5. Bake in centre of oven for 15 minutes, until fluffy and golden brown. Meanwhile, cook sliced green beans, as directed on packet.
6. Serve eggs, with green beans placed around edges of dishes.

French Onion Soup *

For 4 portions:

IMPERIAL	METRIC
¾lb onions	350g onions
2 beef stock cubes	2 beef stock cubes
2 to 4 slices starch-reduced bread	2 to 4 slices starch-reduced bread
2oz Cheddar cheese	50g Cheddar cheese
½ level tablespoon grated Parmesan cheese	1 x 10ml spoon grated Parmesan cheese
Garlic salt (optional)	Garlic salt (optional)
Salt and pepper	Salt and pepper

1. Peel and finely slice onions. Place in a large saucepan, with 750ml (1½ pints) water and stock cubes. Bring to boil, reduce heat, cover and simmer for 15 to 20 minutes, until onion is very tender.
2. Prepare a hot grill and remove grill pan. Toast starch-reduced bread evenly on both sides; cut each slice into quarters. Finely grate Cheddar cheese; place in a basin. Stir in Parmesan cheese, a pinch of garlic salt, if used, and a shake of salt and pepper.
3. When cooked, taste and season soup with salt and pepper, if necessary. Pour soup into a 1-litre (2-pint) ovenproof serving bowl. Float toasted bread pieces on top and sprinkle cheese mixture evenly over surface. Place under grill until cheese has melted and is golden brown. Serve immediately.

Tuna Bake

For 4 portions:

IMPERIAL	METRIC
3 eggs	3 eggs
3 slices starch-reduced brown bread	3 slices starch-reduced brown bread
4oz Edam cheese	100g Edam cheese
4 tomatoes	4 tomatoes
3 rounded tablespoons dried skimmed milk	100ml dried skimmed milk
3 level tablespoons cornflour	3 x 15ml spoons cornflour
1 (7oz) can tuna steak	1 (200g) can tuna steak
1 teaspoon lemon juice	1 x 5ml spoon lemon juice
1 level teaspoon chopped parsley	1 x 5ml spoon chopped parsley
Salt and pepper	Salt and pepper

1. Hard boil eggs for 10 minutes, crack and leave to cool in cold water. Shell and dry on kitchen paper. Cut eggs into quarters.

2. Remove crusts from bread; cut bread into small dice. Grate cheese. Place 2 tomatoes in a bowl; cover with boiling water. Leave for 1 minute, drain, then peel and cut into quarters.

3. Make up dried skimmed milk to 400ml ($\frac{3}{4}$ pint) with water.

4. Place cornflour in a saucepan; blend in milk, a little at a time, bring to boil, stirring. Cook for 2 to 3 minutes, remove from heat.

5. Drain oil from tuna; flake fish with a fork. Add to sauce with half the cheese, eggs, quartered tomatoes, lemon juice and parsley. Taste and season with salt and pepper.

6. Remove rack from grill pan and prepare a moderate grill. Place mixture in a 1 litre ($1\frac{1}{2}$ pint) ovenproof dish. Arrange diced bread over fish mixture and sprinkle with remaining grated cheese. Slice remaining 2 tomatoes thinly; cut each slice in half and arrange the halves around edge of dish.

7. Place dish in grill pan under grill and cook until golden brown.

TUNA BAKE

Potted Mackerel *

For 4 portions:

IMPERIAL	METRIC
1 large (15oz) can mackerel	1 large (425g) can mackerel
4 starch-reduced crispbreads	4 starch-reduced crispbreads
1 small carrot	1 small carrot
1 small onion	1 small onion
1in piece cucumber	2cm piece cucumber
1 teaspoon lemon juice	1 x 5ml spoon lemon juice
½ level teaspoon salt	1 x 2.5ml spoon salt
¼ level teaspoon pepper	½ x 2.5ml spoon pepper
4 level tablespoons low-calorie vinegar and oil dressing	4 x 15ml spoons low-calorie vinegar and oil dressing

GARNISH	GARNISH
1 tomato	1 tomato
Parsley	Parsley

1. Drain mackerel thoroughly and place in a bowl. Flake fish and remove bones. Place crispbreads between 2 sheets of greaseproof paper and crush finely with a rolling pin.
2. Peel and finely grate carrot; peel onion and finely grate 1 x 5ml spoon (1 level teaspoonful). Finely dice cucumber. Add grated carrot and onion, lemon juice, salt, pepper, low-calorie vinegar and oil dressing and crushed crispbread crumbs to mackerel in bowl. Mix together well with a fork, until smooth. Stir in diced cucumber.
3. Press mixture into a 500ml (1-pint) serving dish, or 4 individual pots. Cut tomato into 8 wedges and arrange on top of mixture in dish, with a few sprigs of parsley. Serve with crispbreads or sticks of celery and raw carrot.
NOTE: For a packed lunch, press mixture into a small plastic container with a lid.

Savoury Leeks *

For 4 portions:

4 leeks
4 slices cooked ham
4 slices processed cheese

1. Trim roots, tops and any tough outside leaves from leeks. Cut leeks halfway through lengthwise, then open out and wash thoroughly, to remove any soil. Cook in boiling, salted water for 10 to 12 minutes, until leeks are tender; drain. Prepare a moderate grill.
2. Wrap a slice of ham around each leek. Place in a shallow, ovenproof dish.
3. Cut cheese slices diagonally in halves. Arrange 2 cheese triangles on top of each leek.
4. Grill until cheese melts and turns golden brown. Serve hot.

Breakfast Toasts

For 4 portions:

IMPERIAL	METRIC
6 rashers lean bacon	6 rashers lean bacon
½lb fresh or canned herring roes	¼kg fresh or canned herring roes
1 tomato	1 tomato
4 slices starch-reduced bread	4 slices starch-reduced bread
Low-fat spread	Low-fat spread
Salt and papper	Salt and pepper

1. Prepare a moderate grill. Remove rind and bone from bacon; cut bacon into small pieces. Wash and clean roes (or drain, if canned). Cut tomato into 4 wedges.
2. Fry bacon for 2 to 3 minutes. Add roes and toss in the bacon fat over the heat until golden brown.
3. Toast bread and spread with low-fat spread.
4. Add a shake of salt and pepper to the bacon and roes. Pile mixture on to toast. Garnish each with a tomato wedge.

Cauliflower Soup *

For 4 portions:

IMPERIAL	METRIC
1 (2lb) cauliflower	1 (1kg) cauliflower
2 small onions	2 small onions
1 stick of celery	1 stick of celery
1 medium-sized carrot	1 medium-sized carrot
1 chicken stock cube	1 chicken stock cube
2 pints boiling water	1 litre boiling water
1½ level teaspoons salt	3 x 2.5ml spoons salt
Shake of pepper	Shake of pepper
¼ level teaspoon grated nutmeg	½ x 2.5ml spoons grated nutmeg
1 egg yolk	1 egg yolk
2 tablespoons milk	2 x 15ml spoons milk

1. Wash cauliflower and cut into sprigs, discarding tough outside leaves. Peel and roughly chop onions. Wash and slice celery. Peel and grate carrot. Reserve a little grated carrot for garnish.
2. Dissolve stock cube in boiling water in a large saucepan; add prepared vegetables, salt, pepper and nutmeg. Bring to boil, cover and simmer for 25 to 30 minutes, until vegetables are tender.
3. Sieve soup or liquidise in an electric blender. (Do not over-fill liquidiser goblet; divide soup into 2 or more batches.) Rinse saucepan; return soup to pan.
4. Beat egg yolk and milk together in a basin. Pour a little soup on to egg and milk, mix with a wooden spoon and return to saucepan. Stir over a moderate heat (do not boil) for a few minutes, until slightly thickened. Serve sprinkled with reserved carrot.

Tuna-stuffed Tomatoes *

For 4 portions:

IMPERIAL	METRIC
4 large tomatoes	4 large tomatoes
1 small (3½oz) can tuna	1 small (99g) can tuna
2 level tablespoons low-calorie vinegar and oil dressing	2 x 15ml spoons low-calorie vinegar and oil dressing
1 level teaspoon chopped parsley	1 x 5ml spoon chopped parsley
½ teaspoon lemon juice	1 x 2.5ml spoon lemon juice
½oz (1 slice) starch-reduced breadcrumbs	15g (1 slice) starch-reduced breadcrumbs
¼ level teaspoon salt	½ x 2.5ml spoon salt
Pepper	Pepper

GARNISH	GARNISH
Lettuce leaves	Lettuce leaves
8 cucumber twists	8 cucumber twists
Parsley	Parsley

1. Cut tomatoes in halves; scoop out the insides, using a teaspoon, and place in a sieve over a basin. Leave to drain thoroughly. Discard juice and any hard core, then finely chop pulp.
2. Drain oil from can of tuna; place tuna in a bowl. Add tomato pulp, vinegar and oil dressing, chopped parsley, lemon juice, breadcrumbs, salt and a shake of pepper; mix well.
3. Using a teaspoon, press tuna mixture into tomato shells.
4. Shred lettuce and place on a serving plate. Arrange tomato halves on lettuce and garnish with cucumber twists and sprigs of parsley.

Country Omelet

For 1 portion:

IMPERIAL	METRIC
1 stick of celery	1 stick of celery
1 tomato	1 tomato
4 mushrooms	4 mushrooms
½oz butter	25g butter
2 eggs	2 eggs
½ level teaspoon salt	1 x 2.5ml spoon salt
Pepper	Pepper

1. Wash and chop celery; chop tomato; wash and slice mushrooms.
2. Melt butter in a 23cm (9in) frying pan, add vegetables and cook for about 2 minutes.
3. Beat eggs, salt and a shake of pepper together and pour over vegetables in frying pan. Cook gently until egg has set, about 2 to 3 minutes.
4. Turn out on to a warmed plate and serve immediately.

Melon Cargoes *

For 6 portions:

1 honeydew melon
1 small orange
Ground ginger

1. Cut melon in half; remove seeds with a spoon. Cover each half with self-clinging plastic wrap and place in salad crisper in refrigerator until 10 minutes before meal is to be served.
2. Divide each half of the melon into 3 wedges. With a sharp knife, separate flesh from the skin of melon. Cut flesh across into 5 or 6 pieces.
3. Scrub orange; cut 6 thin slices. Make a cut from peel to centre of each orange slice; twist, to make an 'S' shape. Secure with a cocktail stick and place one on each melon wedge. Serve with ground ginger, and castor sugar for the non-slimmers.

Danish Stuffed Eggs *

For 4 portions:

IMPERIAL	METRIC
4 eggs	4 eggs
Half a bunch of watercress	Half a bunch of watercress
Half a bunch of radishes	Half a bunch of radishes
1 stick of celery	1 stick of celery
1oz Danish Blue cheese	25g Danish Blue cheese
Salt and pepper	Salt and pepper
3 level tablespoons low-calorie vinegar oil dressing	3 x 15ml spoons low-calorie vinegar and oil dressing

1. Hard boil eggs for 10 minutes. Crack and leave to cool in cold water.
2. Remove and discard any discoloured leaves from watercress and trim stalks; wash and drain well. Trim leaves and roots from radishes; wash and drain well. Cut radishes into small dice. Wash celery and cut into 5cm (2in) pieces. Slice each piece into narrow sticks.
3. Shell eggs; but in halves lengthwise and scoop out yolks with a teaspoon. Place yolks in a basin with cheese and a shake of salt and pepper. Beat well with a wooden spoon until smooth.
4. Beat in low-calorie vinegar and oil dressing. Place mixture in a nylon piping bag fitted with a large star tube. Pipe mixture into egg halfes. Alternatively, place in egg halves using teaspoon.
5. Place watercress on a round serving plate. Arrange egg halves in a ring on watercress. Place celery sticks in centre of serving plate and diced radishes around edge of plate, to garnish.
NOTE: For a main course, such as a light lunch, serve 2 eggs (4 halves) per portion.

Clear Vegetable Soup ✻

For 4 portions:

IMPERIAL	METRIC
¼ lb carrots	100g carrots
1 medium-sized onion	1 medium-sized onion
3 sticks of celery	3 sticks of celery
¼ lb cabbage	100g cabbage
2 tomatoes	2 tomatoes
2 chicken extract cubes	2 chicken extract cubes
Salt and pepper	Salt and pepper

1. Peel carrots; cut into thin sticks. Peel and thinly slice onion. Wash celery; cut into thin slices. Wash and finely shred cabbage.

2. Place tomatoes in a basin; cover with boiling water. Leave for 1 minute; drain, then peel. Cut tomatoes in halves; discard seeds and chop flesh.

3. Place chicken extract cubes in a saucepan, with 1 litre (2 pints) water and carrots. Bring to boil; cover and simmer for 5 minutes. Add onion and celery; cook for a further 10 minutes. Add cabbage; cook for a further 5 minutes. Add chopped tomatoes; taste and season with salt and pepper, if necessary. Serve hot.

Egg and Fish Toasts ✻

For 4 portions:

IMPERIAL	METRIC
¼ lb smoked cod or haddock fillet	100g smoked cod or haddock fillet
4 slices starch-reduced bread	4 slices starch-reduced bread
4 tomatoes	4 tomatoes
4 eggs	4 eggs
4oz cottage cheese	100g cottage cheese
1 tablespoon milk	1 x 15ml spoon milk
Salt and pepper	Salt and pepper
Sprigs of parsley	Sprigs of parsley

1. Prepare a moderate grill.

2. Wash fish; place in a saucepan, with a little water. Bring to boil, then immediately reduce heat and cook gently for 5 minutes, or until fish is tender. Drain and flake fish, removing any bones and skin.

3. Toast bread evenly on both sides; grill tomatoes.

4. Place eggs, cottage cheese, milk and some salt and pepper in a basin. Beat together with a fork; turn out into a non-stick saucepan and scramble eggs lightly over a low heat. Stir in fish; heat gently, stirring, for about 1 minute.

5. Divide egg mixture between slices of toast; top each with a sprig of parsley and serve with grilled tomatoes.

BAKED EGGS WITH HAM
(recipe on page 26)

CLEAR VEGETABLE SOUP; EGG AND FISH TOASTS
HAM AND CELERY BAKE

Ham and Celery Bake *

For 4 portions:

IMPERIAL	METRIC
2 sticks of celery	2 sticks of celery
½ level teaspoon salt	1 x 2.5ml spoon salt
1oz Cheddar cheese	25g Cheddar cheese
4 slices cooked ham	4 slices cooked ham
English or French made mustard	English or French made mustard
2 rounded tablespoons dried skimmed milk	4 x 15ml spoons dried skimmed milk
1 egg	1 egg
1 egg yolk	1 egg yolk
Pepper	Pepper

GARNISH	GARNISH
Parsley	Parsley
Tomato wedges	Tomato wedges

1. Prepare a moderate oven (180 deg C, 350 deg F, Gas Mark 4). Pour 1cm (½in) water into a large, shallow roasting tin.
2. Cut 8 pieces of celery, each about 3cm (1½in) long. Cut remaining celery into narrow slices. Place celery in a small saucepan, with 250ml (½ pint) water and salt. Bring to boil, cover and simmer for 5 minutes. Drain well, reserving hot liquor. Grate cheese finely.
3. Cut ham slices in halves lengthwise, to make 8 long strips. Spread each strip lightly on one side with mustard. Place a 3cm (1½in) piece of celery on mustard on each slice; roll up firmly. Arrange rolls in a round, shallow, ½ litre (1-pint) ovenproof dish.
4. Place dried milk in a measuring jug; make up to 250ml (½ pint) with reserved hot liquor. Beat egg and egg yolk together, stir in milk mixture and a shake of pepper. Pour mixture into dish. Sprinkle cheese and remaining celery slices over egg mixture.
5. Place dish in roasting tin and bake in centre of oven for 25 to 30 minutes, until mixture has set and feels firm; remove dish from tin. Sprinkle with chopped parsley.
6. Garnish with a sprig of parsley and tomato wedges. Serve hot or cold, with green beans, lightly boiled celery sticks or green salad.
NOTE: This dish can be made and cooked the day before it is required. Cover with foil or self-clinging plastic wrap and keep in refrigerator. Reheat, if desired.

Baked Eggs with Ham *

(pictured on page 24)

For 4 portions:

IMPERIAL	METRIC
4oz cooked ham or lean bacon	100g cooked ham or lean bacon
4 eggs	4 eggs
4 tablespoons milk	4 x 15ml spoons milk
Salt and pepper	Salt and pepper
Paprika	Paprika

1. Prepare a moderate oven (190 deg C, 375 deg F, Gas Mark 5).
2. Finely shred ham or bacon; divide between 4 individual ovenproof dishes, pressing meat up sides of dishes.
3. Break an egg into each dish; add 1 x 15ml spoon (1 tablespoon) of milk to each and sprinkle with some salt and a shake of pepper.
4. Place dishes on a baking sheet and cook on shelf in top position of oven for 12 to 15 minutes, depending on how set you want the eggs. Sprinkle with paprika; serve hot.

Vichyssoise

For 4 portions:

IMPERIAL	METRIC
½ lb potatoes	¼ kg potatoes
1 medium-sized leek	1 medium-sized leek
1 chicken stock cube	1 chicken stock cube
1 rounded tablespoon dried skimmed milk	2 x 15ml spoons dried skimmed milk
Salt	Salt
Pepper	Pepper

GARNISH	GARNISH
Chopped chives or chopped parsley	Chopped chives or chopped parsley

1. Peel potatoes; cut into small cubes. Trim root, most of green top and any tough outside leaves from leek. Cut leek halfway through lengthwise, then open out and wash thoroughly, to remove any soil; finely slice into rings.
2. Place potatoes and leek in a medium-sized saucepan with stock cube and 450ml (¾ pint) water. Bring to boil, cover and simmer for 25 to 30 minutes, until leek is tender.
3. Press soup through a sieve into a large bowl, or place contents of pan in a liquidiser goblet and run machine until mixture is well blended. (Do not over-fill liquidiser goblet; divide soup into 2 or more batches.) Place soup in a large bowl.
4. Place dried skimmed milk in a measuring jug and make up to 300ml (½ pint) with cold water; stir into soup.

5. Cover bowl with foil or self-clinging plastic wrap. Leave until cool; chill thoroughly. Just before serving, taste and season with salt and white pepper; serve, sprinkled with a few chopped chives or a little chopped parsley.

NOTE: Serve soup hot, if desired: Rinse saucepan; return soup to saucepan. Add reconstituted dried skimmed milk and reheat gently. Taste and season with salt and pepper and serve, sprinkled with a few chopped chives or chopped parsley.

Savoury-topped Mushrooms *

For 4 portions:

IMPERIAL	METRIC
8 large open mushrooms	8 large open mushrooms
Oil	Oil
4 rashers lean bacon	4 rashers lean bacon
4 eggs	4 eggs
2 tablespoons milk	2 x 15ml spoons milk
Salt and black pepper	Salt and black pepper

1. Prepare a moderate grill. Wash mushrooms and remove stalks. Brush mushroom caps with oil and place on grill rack. Grill for 2 to 3 minutes on each side; place on a serving dish and keep warm.
2. Remove rind and bone from bacon; chop bacon. Chop mushroom stalks. Place chopped bacon and mushroom in a saucepan and fry for 2 to 3 minutes.
3. Beat eggs, milk, salt and pepper together in a bowl. Pour on to mushroom mixture in saucepan. Cook until egg just thickens, stirring continuously.
4. Pile on to mushroom caps and serve hot.

Egg and Spinach Grill *

For 4 portions:

IMPERIAL	METRIC
2 (8oz) cartons frozen leaf spinach	2 (227g) cartons frozen leaf spinach
8oz cottage cheese	200g cottage cheese
4 eggs	4 eggs
Salt and pepper	Salt and pepper

1. Cook spinach, as directed on carton. Drain in a sieve and press, to remove excess water.
2. Prepare a moderate grill; remove rack from grill pan. Divide spinach mixture equally between 4 individual ovenproof dishes. Form into 'nests' with back of a spoon.
3. Divide cottage cheese between dishes; place in grill pan and heat for 2 minutes. Break an egg on to cottage cheese in each dish; sprinkle with a little salt and pepper. Place under grill for about 6 to 8 minutes, until egg is set and lightly browned. Serve with starch-reduced bread or crispbread, low-fat spread and salad, if desired.

Mushroom Aspic Moulds ✱

For 6 portions:

IMPERIAL	METRIC
1 small (7½oz) can mushrooms	1 small (212g) can mushrooms
1 level tablespoon gelatine	1 x 15ml spoon gelatine
1 pint tomato juice	½ litre tomato juice
½ level teaspoon celery salt	1 x 2.5ml spoon celery salt
½ level teaspoon dried basil	1 x 2.5ml spoon dried basil
Sprigs of watercress	Sprigs of watercress
Cucumber slices	Cucumber slices

1. Drain liquor from can of mushrooms; reserve 3 x 15ml spoons (3 tablespoons) in a large basin. Sprinkle gelatine over surface and leave to soften.
2. Thinly slice mushrooms. Place tomato juice, celery salt and basil in a small saucepan. Bring to boil, reduce heat and cook for 5 minutes. Add to basin and stir until gelatine has dissolved; stir in mushrooms.
3. Leave to cool, then chill until just on the point of setting. Stir, then ladle into 6, 125ml (4 fluid oz) moulds or cups; chill until firm.
4. To serve: Dip moulds into very hot water and turn out on to 6 small plates. Garnish with watercress and slices of cucumber.

Cucumber Cocktail Soup ✱

(pictured on page 28)

For 4 portions:

IMPERIAL	METRIC
1 small onion	1 small onion
Half a medium-sized cucumber (about 6oz)	Half a medium-sized cucumber (about 150g)
1 teaspoon oil	1 x 5ml spoon oil
¼ level teaspoon dried basil	½ x 2.5ml spoon dried basil
Celery salt	Celery salt
1 chicken stock cube	1 chicken stock cube
½ pint boiling water	250ml boiling water
Half a small bay leaf	Half a small bay leaf
1 teaspoon Worcestershire sauce	1 x 5ml spoon Worcestershire sauce
Salt and pepper	Salt and pepper
1 (19 fluid oz) can tomato juice	1 (540ml) can tomato juice

1. Peel and finely chop onion. Dice cucumber finely.
2. Heat oil in a medium-sized saucepan. Add onion, diced cucumber, basil and a shake of celery salt. Fry gently for 2 minutes, stirring.
3. Dissolve stock cube in boiling water; add to saucepan, with bay leaf, Worcestershire sauce, ½ x 2.5ml spoon (¼ level teaspoon) salt and a shake of pepper. Bring to boil, stirring; simmer for 5 minutes. Leave to cool. Chill tomato juice.

4. Pour soup into a chilled soup tureen and add tomato juice; remove bay leaf. Taste and add more salt and pepper, if necessary. Leave in refrigerator until ready to serve. Just before serving, skim off any oil with kitchen paper.
NOTE: Serve hot, if desired.

Open Sandwiches

(pictured on page 28)

For 4 portions:

IMPERIAL	METRIC
1 (3½oz) can red salmon	1 (99g) can red salmon
Low-calorie vinegar and oil dressing	Low-calorie vinegar and oil dressing
Lemon juice	Lemon juice
Salt and pepper	Salt and pepper
1 hard-boiled egg	1 hard-boiled egg
4 gherkins	4 gherkins
2 medium-sized tomatoes	2 medium-sized tomatoes
2in piece of cucumber	5cm piece of cucumber
8 slices starch-reduced crispbread	8 slices starch-reduced crispbread
Low-fat spread	Low-fat spread
Watercress	Watercress
Lettuce	Lettuce
2oz Edam cheese, grated	50g Edam cheese, grated
4 stuffed olives	4 stuffed olives

1. Drain liquor from can of salmon; place salmon in a basin and remove any skin and bone. Add 2 x 10ml spoons (2 rounded teaspoons) low-calorie dressing, 1 x 2.5ml spoon (½ teaspoon) lemon juice, a pinch of salt and a shake of pepper; mix well.
2. Cut hard-boiled egg into 8 slices. Cut gherkins into fans, by making 4 cuts in each gherkin almost through to stalk end. Cut each tomato into 6 wedges. Cut 6 thin slices from cucumber.
3. Spread crispbread lightly with low-fat spread. Divide salmon mixture equally between 4 crispbreads; place a slice of hard-boiled egg on each. Cut 4 cucumber slices through to centre, twist; arrange one next to each egg slice. Arrange 2 wedges of tomato next to cucumber; place half a slice of cucumber in between. Garnish with watercress.
4. Cut remaining cucumber, slices of hard-boiled egg and tomato wedges into small dice. Place in a basin, with 1 x 10ml spoon (1 rounded teaspoon) low-calorie dressing, a few drops of lemon juice, a pinch of salt and a shake of pepper; mix well.
5. Arrange a small lettuce leaf on each of the remaining 4 slices of crispbread. Place a pile of grated cheese at one end of each crispbread, and egg mixture at the other end. Garnish with gherkin fans, clises of stuffed olive and watercress.
6. Arrange crispbread on a wooden board or plate.

CUCUMBER COCKTAIL SOUP
OPEN SANDWICHES
(recipe on page 27)

MAIN COURSE DISHES

Marrow with Meatballs

(pictured on front cover)

For 4 portions:

IMPERIAL	METRIC
½ lb onions	¼ kg onions
2 sticks of celery	2 sticks of celery
1 medium-sized marrow	1 medium-sized marrow
1 egg	1 egg
Garlic salt	Garlic salt
Salt and pepper	Salt and pepper
1lb lean minced beef	½ kg lean minced beef
Plain flour	Plain flour
2 teaspoons oil	1 x 10ml spoon oil
½ level teaspoon mixed dried herbs	1 x 2.5ml spoon mixed dried herbs
2 teaspoons Worcestershire sauce	1 x 10ml spoon Worcestershire sauce
1 large green pepper	1 large green pepper
2 large tomatoes	2 large tomatoes

1. Prepare a moderate oven (190 deg C, 375 deg F, Gas Mark 5).

2. Prepare vegetables: peel and slice onions; wash celery and thinly slice; peel marrow, discard seeds and cut marrow into 2cm (1in) cubes.

3. Place egg in a basin, add a shake of garlic salt, 1 x 2.5ml spoon (½ level teaspoon) salt and ½ x 2.5ml spoon (¼ level teaspoon) pepper; mix together. Add meat to egg mixture and mix thoroughly. Lightly flour hands. Divide meat mixture; roll between palms of hands, to make 32 meatballs.

4. Heat oil in a large saucepan. Fry meatballs for 5 minutes, turning frequently, until well browned. Remove from pan and drain on kitchen paper.

5. Add onion to pan; cook until almost transparent. Add celery, marrow, 1 x 5ml spoon (1 level teaspoon) salt, mixed dried herbs, ½ x 2.5ml spoon (¼ level teaspoon pepper) and Worcestershire sauce. Bring to boil, stirring; cover with a lid and simmer for 10 minutes, until marrow is almost tender.

6. Turn out into a shallow, 1½-litre (3-pint) oven-proof dish and place meatballs on top. Cover dish with a lid or foil and cook on shelf in top position of oven for 40 minutes.

7. Finely slice pepper into rings; discard seeds, core and white pith. Place pepper in a small saucepan, cover with cold water and bring to boil. Cook for 2 minutes, then remove pepper from pan. Remove pan from heat, add tomatoes and leave for 1 minute. Drain, peel, then cut into wedges.

8. Remove lid or foil from marrow mixture; stir in green pepper and tomato wedges. Replace foil and cook dish for a further 20 minutes. Serve piping hot.

Chicken with Orange ✱

For 4 portions:

IMPERIAL	METRIC
2 oranges	2 oranges
1oz shelled almonds	25g shelled almonds
4 chicken joints	4 chicken joints
Oil	Oil
Salt and pepper	Salt and pepper
Watercress	Watercress

1. Scrub orange. Using a sharp knife or potato peeler, cut peel from one orange, taking care not to include any white pith. Cut into very thin strips. Squeeze juice from both oranges.

2. Remove rack from grill pan and prepare a moderate grill. Place almonds in a basin and cover with boiling water; leave for 1 minute. Drain; remove skins. Place almonds in grill pan and grill until browned.

3. Place chicken joints in grill pan; brush with a little oil and sprinkle with salt and pepper. Grill for 20 to 30 minutes, turning once, until golden brown.

4. Remove chicken joints and arrange on a serving dish; keep warm. Add orange juice, rind and the almonds to grill pan. Heat under grill for about 1 minute.

5. Pour the dressing over chicken joints, garnish with watercress and serve with a green salad.

Kidney Casserole ✱

For 4 portions:

IMPERIAL	METRIC
½ lb carrots	¼ kg carrots
2 sticks of celery	2 sticks of celery
½ lb onions	¼ kg onions
2oz mushrooms	50g mushrooms
1 beef stock cube	1 beef stock cube
½ pint boiling water	250ml boiling water
1lb lambs' kidneys	½ kg lambs' kidneys
1 level teaspoon curry powder	1 x 5ml spoon curry powder
Salt	Salt

1. Prepare a moderate oven (180 deg C, 350 deg F, Gas Mark 4).

2. Scrape carrots, wash celery, peel onions and wash mushrooms. Finely slice carrots, celery and onions. Cut mushrooms in halves. Dissolve stock cube in boiling water.

3. Cut kidneys in halves; remove skin and core. Place in a 1¼-litre (2-pint) casserole. Sprinkle with curry powder and ½ x 2.5ml spoon (¼ level teaspoon) salt. Add vegetables and stock; cover and cook for 45 minutes, until kidney is tender. Taste and season with more salt, if necessary. Serve casserole with Brussels sprouts.

Sweet and Sour Chicken *

For 4 portions:

IMPERIAL	METRIC
4 chicken joints	4 chicken joints
1 green pepper	1 green pepper
1 medium-sized onion	1 medium-sized onion
1 small (8½oz) can pineapple pieces	1 small (240g) can pineapple pieces
1 tablespoon soy sauce	1 x 15ml spoon soy sauce
1 tablespoon vinegar	1 x 15ml spoon vinegar
1 small (8oz) can tomatoes	1 small (226g) can tomatoes
¾ level teaspoon salt	1 x 2.5ml spoon salt
2 sugar substitute tablets	2 sugar substitute tablets

1. Prepare a moderate oven (190 deg C, 375 deg F, Gas Mark 5).
2. Remove skin from chicken joints. Place joints in a 1½-litre (3-pint) casserole and cook, uncovered, in the oven for 30 minutes.
3. Cut pepper in half lengthwise; discard seeds, core and white pith; slice pepper finely. Peel and slice onion. Drain pineapple; place in a saucepan with onion, green pepper, soy sauce, vinegar, contents of can of tomatoes, 250ml (½ pint) water, salt and sugar substitute tablets. Bring to boil, stirring; cover and simmer for 20 minutes.
4. Pour sauce over chicken in the oven and cook for a further 30 minutes, or until chicken is cooked, basting occasionally with the sauce. Serve with boiled rice, if desired, and a green vegetable.

Liver in Yoghourt Sauce

For 4 portions:

IMPERIAL	METRIC
1 large onion	1 large onion
1 teaspoon oil	1 x 5ml spoon oil
1 small (8oz) can tomatoes	1 small (226g) can tomatoes
½ level teaspoon salt	1 x 2.5ml spoon salt
Pinch of Cayenne pepper	Pinch of Cayenne pepper
1 level teaspoon yeast extract	1 x 5ml spoon yeast extract
1 bay leaf	1 bay leaf
1lb lambs' liver	½ kg lambs' liver
¼ lb button mushrooms	100g button mushrooms
8oz long-grain rice	200g long-grain rice
1 (5.3 oz) carton natural low-fat yoghourt	1 (150g) carton natural low-fat yoghourt
Chopped parsley	Chopped parsley

1. Peel and chop onion. Fry onion in oil in a saucepan for 5 minutes.
2. Add contents of can of tomatoes, salt, Cayenne pepper, yeast extract and bay leaf. Bring to boil and cook quickly for 5 to 6 minutes, to reduce liquid by half.
3. Cut liver into thin strips, discarding any gristle. Wash mushrooms. Add liver and mushrooms to saucepan; cover and simmer for 6 to 7 minutes.
4. Meanwhile, cook rice in a large saucepan of boiling, salted water for 12 minutes. Test by pressing a grain between thumb and finger. Drain and rinse with hot water. Arrange rice in a border around edge of a warmed serving plate.
5. Remove bay leaf from liver mixture. Pour liver mixture into centre of rice. Pour yoghourt over liver and sprinkle with chopped parsley. Serve immediately.

Kidney Lorraine

For 4 portions:

IMPERIAL	METRIC
8 lambs' kidneys	8 lambs' kidneys
Half a green pepper	Half a green pepper
1 onion	1 onion
4oz lean bacon	100g lean bacon
4oz mushrooms	100g mushrooms
½ oz margarine	25g margarine
¾ pint stock or water	350ml stock or water
2 rounded teaspoons tomato purée	2 x 10ml spoons tomato purée
Salt and pepper	Salt and pepper
2 rounded teaspoons cornflour	2 x 10ml spoons cornflour
1 tablespoon dry sherry (optional)	1 x 15ml spoon dry sherry (optional)
2 tablespoons yoghourt	2 x 15ml spoons yoghourt

1. Remove fat and skin from kidneys; halve, remove core and cut into quarters.
2. Cut pepper in half lengthwise; discard seeds, core and white pith. Cut pepper into strips. Place in a small saucepan, cover with cold water and bring to boil. Cook for 5 minutes; drain.
3. Peel and chop onion. Remove rind from bacon; cut bacon into thin strips. Wash mushrooms and cut into quarters.
4. Melt margarine in a frying pan and fry bacon and onion for 2 to 3 minutes. Add kidneys and fry for 3 minutes.
5. Stir in stock or water, tomato purée and some salt and pepper; bring to boil.
6. Blend cornflour with a little cold water and stir into frying pan. Add sherry, if used, mushrooms and green pepper. Reduce heat, cover and cook slowly for 15 minutes or until kidney is tender.
7. Taste and season with more salt and pepper, if necessary; pour into a warmed serving dish. Beat yoghourt until it is of pouring consistency, then lightly stir into dish just before serving.

Braised Beef with Tomatoes *

For 4 portions:

IMPERIAL	METRIC
1¼lb chuck steak	½kg chuck steak
1 medium-sized onion	1 medium-sized onion
1 level teaspoon salt	1 x 5ml spoon salt
1 level teaspoon paprika	1 x 5ml spoon paprika
1 bay leaf	1 bay leaf
1 large (14oz) can tomatoes	1 large (396g) can tomatoes
4 medium-sized potatoes	4 medium-sized potatoes
8 rounded teaspoons natural low-fat yoghourt	8 x 10ml spoons natural low-fat yoghourt
Chives, to garnish	Chives, to garnish

1. Prepare a moderate oven (180 deg C, 350 deg F, Gas Mark 4). Trim any excess fat from meat; cut meat into 4 portions.

2. Peel and thinly slice onion. Place a large frying pan over a moderate heat; when hot, place 2 pieces of meat in pan for about 1 minute, until browned. Turn and brown other side; place in a shallow, oven-proof dish. Repeat with remainder of meat. As meat may stick slightly to pan, it is advisable to use a non-stick pan, if available (add meat to cold pan).

3. Place onion in frying pan and stir for 1 minute; spread over meat. Add salt, paprika and bay leaf. Pour contents of can of tomatoes over meat and onions, cover with a lid or foil and bake just above centre of oven for about 2 hours, until meat is tender. Remove bay leaf.

4. Scrub potatoes and prick well with a fork. Place on same shelf as meat. Bake for 2 hours. Just before serving, cut a cross in the top of each potato and press gently at base to open. Top each with 2 rounded teaspoons of yoghourt and some chives. Serve immediately with large helpings of cabbage.

NOTE: If on reducing diet, include potato only as part of daily allowance, if desired.

BRAISED BEEF WITH TOMATOES

Ox Liver Casserole *

For 4 portions:

IMPERIAL	METRIC
1lb ox liver	½ kg ox liver
½ lb onions	¼ kg onions
Half a large red or green pepper	Half a large red or green pepper
1 beef stock cube	1 beef stock cube
½ pint boiling water	250ml boiling water
1 teaspoon soy sauce	1 x 5ml spoon soy sauce
Salt and pepper	Salt and pepper
Half a bay leaf	Half a bay leaf

1. Prepare a moderate oven (180 deg C, 350 deg F, Gas Mark 4). Wash liver and cut into 4 equal-sized pieces; place in a shallow, 1¼-litre (2-pint) oven-proof serving dish.
2. Peel and finely slice onions; place on liver. Finely slice pepper and place on top of onions.
3. Dissolve stock cube in boiling water. Add soy sauce and pour over liver and vegetables in dish. Add ½ x 2.5ml spoon (¼ level teaspoon) salt, a few shakes of pepper and halved bay leaf. Cover with foil or a lid and cook in centre of oven for 35 to 40 minutes, until liver is tender.
4. Remove bay leaf. Taste and season with more salt and pepper, if necessary. Serve immediately with Parsleyed Turnips (recipe on page 72) and peas.

Liver in Tomato Sauce *

For 4 portions:

IMPERIAL	METRIC
1lb lambs' liver	½ kg lambs' liver
Salt	Salt
Black pepper	Black pepper
1 (15oz) can tomato juice	1 (425g) can tomato juice
2 teaspoons cider vinegar	1 x 10ml spoon cider vinegar
1 level teaspoon dry mustard	1 x 5ml spoon dry mustard
1 level tablespoon dried, sliced onion	1 x 15ml spoon dried, sliced onion
2 drops liquid sweetener	2 drops liquid sweetener
½ level tablespoon chopped parsley	1 x 10ml spoon chopped parsley

1. Trim liver; cut into 5cm by 2cm (2in by ½ in) strips. Place in a medium-sized saucepan, with 25ml (¼ pint) water, ½ x 2.5ml spoon (¼ level teaspoon) salt and a little black pepper. Bring to boil and cook for 10 to 12 minutes, until liver is tender.
2. Remove liver from pan, using a draining spoon.

Place on a warmed serving plate; keep hot. Add tomato juice, vinegar, mustard and dried onion to pan. Bring to boil and boil rapidly until sauce is reduced and thick, about 8 minutes.
3. Stir in liquid sweetener; taste and season with more salt and pepper, if necessary. Pour sauce over liver; sprinkle with chopped parsley. Serve immediately, with cauliflower and peas.

Fish Dolmas with Mushrooms *

For 4 portions:

IMPERIAL	METRIC
6 large cabbage leaves	6 large cabbage leaves
1 (7oz) can mackerel or tuna in oil	1 (200g) can mackerel or tuna in oil
Lemon juice	Lemon juice
½ level teaspoon mixed dried herbs	1 x 2.5ml spoon mixed dried herbs
1 rounded tablespoon tomato purée	2 x 15ml spoons tomato purée
1oz starch-reduced breadcrumbs	25g starch-reduced breadcrumbs
Salt and pepper	Salt and pepper
1 small (8oz) can tomatoes	1 small (226g) can tomatoes
Garlic salt (optional)	Garlic salt (optional)
4oz mushrooms	100g mushrooms
1 level teaspoon chopped parsley	1 x 5ml spoon chopped parsley

1. Prepare a moderate oven (180 deg C, 350 deg F, Gas Mark 4). Wash cabbage leaves; cook in boiling, salted water for 5 minutes, then drain.
2. Drain oil from can of fish; place fish in a basin and remove any bones. Add 1 x 5ml spoon (1 teaspoon) lemon juice, mixed dried herbs, tomato purée, breadcrumbs, 1 x 2.5ml spoon (½ level teaspoon) salt and a shake of pepper. Mix together well.
3. Divide fish mixture evenly between cabbage leaves; roll each cabbage leaf around and tuck ends neatly under (if necessary, tie with fine string or cotton.) Place in a shallow, ovenproof serving dish.
4. Empty contents of can of tomatoes over stuffed cabbage leaves. Sprinkle with a little salt, pepper and garlic salt, if used. Cover dish with a lid or foil; cook in centre of oven for 45 to 50 minutes.
5. Wash and slice mushrooms. Place in a saucepan with a lid; add 1 x 5ml spoon (1 teaspoon) lemon juice and a shake of salt and pepper.
6. Bring to boil, cover with a lid and cook for 2 minutes, stirring occasionally. Remove from heat and stir in chopped parsley; keep hot.
7. To serve: Remove string, if used. Serve dolmas with mushrooms.

Bacon Plaice Kebabs

For 4 portions:

IMPERIAL	METRIC
2 onions	2 onions
1lb courgettes	½kg courgettes
¾lb tomatoes	350g tomatoes
1 tablespoon oil	1 x 15ml spoon oil
Salt and pepper	Salt and pepper
12 small plaice fillets	12 small plaice fillets
6 rashers lean bacon	6 rashers lean bacon
Butter	Butter

1. Peel and slice onions. Wash and thinly slice courgettes. Place tomatoes in a bowl; cover with boiling water and leave for 1 minute. Drain, peel and cut into slices.
2. Heat oil in a saucepan; fry onions for 5 minutes.
3. Cover onions with courgettes and lay tomatoes on top. Sprinkle well with salt and pepper. Cover saucepan with a tight-fitting lid and cook for 30 minutes over a low heat.
4. Remove dark skin from plaice fillets and roll up, skinned side inside.
5. Remove rind from bacon; spread each rasher flat with the back of a knife. Cut each rasher in half and roll up. Arrange 3 fillets of plaice and 3 bacon rolls alternately on each of 4 skewers.
6. Prepare a moderate grill. Remove rack from grill pan and melt a little butter in grill pan.
7. Place skewers in grill pan and grill for 4 to 5 minutes, until cooked, basting occasionally and turning once. Arrange vegetables on a warmed serving dish and place skewers on top.

NOTE: If courgettes are not available, use sliced cucumber.

Soufflé Beef Layer ✳

(pictured on page 36)

For 4 portions:

IMPERIAL	METRIC
1 small onion	1 small onion
1lb lean minced beef	½kg lean minced beef
1 rounded tablespoon chopped parsley	2 x 15ml spoons chopped parsley
Salt and pepper	Salt and pepper
2 eggs	2 eggs
3 rounded tablespoons mixed, cooked vegetables (peas, sweet corn, green beans, diced carrots or celery)	100ml mixed, cooked vegetables (peas, sweet corn, green beans, diced carrots or celery)

1. Prepare a moderate oven (180 deg C, 350 deg F, Gas Mark 4).
2. Peel and grate onion into a bowl. Add minced beef, parsley, 1 x 5ml spoon (1 level teaspoon) salt and a shake of pepper. Separate eggs; place whites in a clean, grease-free bowl. Add one yolk to beef and mix well. Place other yolk in a basin, add a little salt and pepper and mix well.
3. Press beef into an 20cm (8in) round on an oven-proof plate; cover with foil. Bake in centre of oven for 35 to 40 minutes; remove foil.
4. Whisk egg whites until stiff, but not dry. Add a little egg white to yolk; mix well, then fold into egg whites, using a metal spoon. Lightly fold in vegetables, pile on beef, return to oven and cook for a further 15 minutes. Serve soufflé hot with a green vegetable.

Meaty Cabbage Layer

(pictured on page 37)

For 4 portions:

IMPERIAL	METRIC
1 medium-sized onion	1 medium-sized onion
¼lb lambs' liver	100g lambs' liver
¾lb lean minced beef	300g lean minced beef
Pinch of mixed dried herbs	Pinch of mixed dried herbs
1 small (8oz) can tomatoes	1 small (226g) can tomatoes
Salt and pepper	Salt and pepper
Cornflour	Cornflour
1½lb firm cabbage	¾kg firm cabbage
4oz Cheddar cheese	100g Cheddar cheese
3 rounded tablespoons dried skimmed milk	6 x 15ml spoons dried skimmed milk

1. Peel onion; cut into small pieces. Mince liver and onion. Place minced beef, liver and onion in a saucepan over a moderate heat; cook, stirring occasionally, for 5 minutes. Add herbs, contents of can of tomatoes and some salt and pepper. Continue cooking for a further 10 minutes.
2. Blend 1 x 10ml spoon (2 level teaspoons) cornflour with 1 x 15ml spoon (1 tablespoon) water; stir into meat mixture and cook for 3 minutes.
3. Meanwhile, wash and shred cabbage. Cook cabbage in boiling, salted water for 8 to 10 minutes, until just tender; drain well.
4. Grate cheese. Place 3 x 15ml spoons (3 level tablespoons) cornflour in a saucepan. Make dried skimmed milk up to 375ml (¾ pint) with water; gradually blend milk into cornflour. Bring to boil, stirring; cook for 3 minutes. Stir in two-thirds of the cheese; taste and season with salt and pepper.
5. Prepare a moderate grill. Place half the cabbage in base of a warmed ovenproof dish; pour half the sauce over. Spread meat mixture over sauce; cover with remaining cabbage and top with remaining sauce. Sprinkle with remaining cheese.
6. Grill until cheese is golden brown. Serve hot with carrots and green beans.

SOUFFLE BEEF LAYER
(recipe on page 35)

MEATY CABBAGE LAYER
(recipe on page 35)

Foil-baked Whiting ✱

For 4 portions:

IMPERIAL	METRIC
2 large or 4 small whiting	2 large or 4 small whiting
4 starch-reduced crispbreads	4 starch-reduced crispbreads
2 level teaspoons chopped parsley	1 x 10ml spoon chopped parsley
Grated rind of half a lemon	Grated rind of half a lemon
1 teaspoon lemon juice	1 x 5ml spoon lemon juice
½ teaspoon salt	1 x 2.5ml spoon salt
Black pepper	Black pepper

1. Prepare a moderate oven (190 deg C, 375 deg F, Gas Mark 5).

2. Cut heads and fins off whiting, using a sharp knife. Cut along underside of each fish, from head to tail. Scrape away any gut and blood vessels and discard. Wash under cold water and dry on kitchen paper. Place fish on a large piece of foil on a baking sheet.

3. To make stuffing: Place crispbreads between 2 sheets of greaseproof paper; crush finely with a rolling pin. Place in a basin; add parsley, lemon rind and juice, salt and a little black pepper. Mix together.

4. Press stuffing into fish; sprinkle any remaining stuffing over fish. Bring foil over fish and fold edges together, to make a parcel. Place in centre of oven; bake for 20 to 25 minutes, depending on size of fish. Serve with cabbage or spinach.

Haddock and Cheese Crumble

For 4 portions:

IMPERIAL	METRIC
1 small onion	1 small onion
2 sticks of celery	2 sticks of celery
4oz Cheddar cheese	100g Cheddar cheese
1¼lb haddock fillet	½kg haddock fillet
2 level tablespoons plain flour	2 x 15ml spoons plain flour
Salt and pepper	Salt and pepper
2oz fresh white starch-reduced breadcrumbs	50g fresh white starch-reduced breadcrumbs
1oz margarine	25g margarine
1 large (14oz) can tomatoes	1 large (396g) can tomatoes

1. Prepare a moderate oven (190 deg C, 375 deg F, Gas Mark 5).

2. Peel and finely chop onion; wash and slice celery; grate cheese. Wash haddock and remove skin; cut into pieces. Mix flour and some salt and pepper together on a plate. Coat haddock in seasoned flour. Mix breadcrumbs, grated cheese and some salt and pepper together.

3. Melt margarine in a frying pan. Add onion and celery and cook for 3 minutes, until onion is tender. Add haddock to pan and turn carefully until browned. Turn into a 1-litre (2-pint) casserole. Add tomatoes to pan and bring to boil, stirring; pour over fish mixture. Cover with breadcrumb and cheese mixture.

4. Bake in centre of oven for 40 to 45 minutes, until golden brown. Serve hot with green beans.

Mackerel with Barbecue Sauce ✱

For 4 portions:

IMPERIAL	METRIC
BARBECUE SAUCE	BARBECUE SAUCE
2 medium-sized onions	2 medium-sized onions
½oz margarine	25g margarine
3 drops liquid sweetener	3 drops liquid sweetener
½ level teaspoon dry mustard	1 x 2.5ml spoon dry mustard
¼ level teaspoon pepper	½ x 2.5 ml spoon pepper
1 tablespoon Worcester sauce	1 x 15ml spoon Worcester sauce
3 level tablespoons tomato ketchup	3 x 15ml spoons tomato ketchup
3 teaspoons vinegar	1 x 15ml spoon vinegar
4 medium-sized mackerel	4 medium-sized mackerel

1. Peel and chop onions. Melt margarine in a frying pan over a moderate heat; add onions and fry, without browning, until almost soft. Add remaining sauce ingredients and 4 x 15ml spoons (4 tablespoons) water; bring to boil and cook gently for 5 minutes.

2. Prepare a moderate grill.

3. Cut heads and fins off mackerel, using a sharp knife. Cut along underside of each fish, from head to tail. Scrape away any gut and blood vessels and discard. Wash under cold water and dry on kitchen paper. Score 3 diagonal slits across skin on both sides. Place fish on grill rack and cook for 8 to 10 minutes on each side, then place on a warmed serving dish.

4. Reheat sauce and spoon a little over each mackerel. Serve with small portions of creamed potato and peas, or salad.

Poached Haddock ✱

For 4 to 6 portions:

IMPERIAL	METRIC
2lb tail-end piece of fresh haddock or cod	1kg tail-end piece of fresh haddock or cod
2 medium-sized lemons	2 medium-sized lemons
½ level teaspoon mixed dried herbs	1 x 2.5ml spoon mixed dried herbs
½ level teaspoon salt	1 x 2.5ml spoon salt
Pepper	Pepper
Sprigs of parsley	Sprigs of parsley

1. Wash fish; dry on kitchen paper.
2. Scrub lemons; squeeze juice from one lemon and place in a measuring jug. Cut remaining lemon into 4 or 6 wedges and reserve for garnish.
3. Make lemon juice up to 250ml (½ pint) with water; pour into a large frying pan or flameproof dish. Add herbs, salt and a shake of pepper, then bring to boil.
4. Place fish in frying pan or flameproof dish; cover with foil or a lid. Poach very gently for 15 to 20 minutes, until fish is tender.
5. Remove fish carefully from pan and place on a warmed serving dish. Garnish with lemon wedges and sprigs of parsley. Serve with low-calorie vinegar and oil dressing, if desired, and green beans or broccoli.

Cauliflower Meat Pie

(pictured on page 40)

For 4 portions:

IMPERIAL	METRIC
1½lb lean minced beef	¾kg lean minced beef
1 medium-sized onion	1 medium-sized onion
1 meat extract cube	1 meat extract cube
1 tablespoon Worcester sauce	1 x 15ml spoon Worcester sauce
1 small (8oz) can tomatoes	1 small (226g) can tomatoes
1 level teaspoon cornflour	1 x 5ml spoon cornflour
Salt and pepper	Salt and pepper
1 medium-sized cauliflower	1 medium-sized cauliflower
¼ pint milk	125ml milk
2oz Cheddar cheese	50g Cheddar cheese

1. Place meat in a large saucepan. Peel and chop onion; add to meat. Cook over a low heat, stirring, for about 10 minutes, until meat has browned slightly. Drain off any excess fat.
2. Crumble and add meat extract cube, Worcester sauce and contents of can of tomatoes. Blend cornflour with 1 x 15ml spoon (1 tablespoon) cold water; stir into meat mixture, with 1 x 5ml spoon (1 level teaspoon) salt and a shake of pepper. Bring to boil; cover and simmer for 15 minutes.
3. Break cauliflower into florets; cook in boiling, salted water until tender, about 10 minutes. Drain cauliflower, mash with a potato masher. Stir in milk 1 x 5ml spoon (1 level teaspoon) salt and a shake of pepper; beat well with a wooden spoon.
4. Prepare a moderate grill. Place meat mixture in an ovenproof dish. Cover with the mashed cauliflower. Grate cheese; sprinkle over cauliflower. Grill until golden brown, about 5 minutes. Serve hot, with cabbage and carrots.

Italian Meat Roll

(pictured on page 41)

For 4 portions:

IMPERIAL	METRIC
8 medium-sized onions	8 medium-sized onions
1lb lean minced beef	½kg lean minced beef
1 egg	1 egg
Pinch of mixed dried herbs	Pinch of mixed dried herbs
Salt and pepper	Salt and pepper
1 hard-boiled egg	1 hard-boiled egg
2oz salami	50g salami
4oz cottage cheese	100g cottage cheese
1 level teaspoon chopped parsley	1 x 5ml spoon chopped parsley
Oil	Oil
4 tomatoes	4 tomatoes
Parsley to garnish	Parsley to garnish

1. Prepare a moderate oven (190 deg C, 375 deg F, Gas Mark 5). Cut a piece of foil, 27cm by 20cm (11in by 8in).
2. Peel onions, place in a saucepan and cover with water. Bring to boil, cover and simmer for 10 minutes; drain, reserving stock for gravy or a soup, if desired.
3. Place minced beef, egg, herbs, 1 x 2.5ml spoon (½ level teaspoon) salt and a shake of pepper in a bowl. Mix well with a fork. Turn out on to foil and press out to an oblong, 22cm by 15cm (9in by 6in).
4. Peel and chop hard-boiled egg, peel off salami skin and cut salami into small dice; place egg and salami in a bowl with cottage cheese, parsley and a little salt and pepper. Mix well with a fork.
5. Spread stuffing down the centre of meat, from one long side to the other. Roll up meat mixture in foil, enclosing stuffing, and joining beef underneath. Press foil together at each end of roll. Place roll in a roasting tin. Arrange onions around meat roll and lightly brush with a little oil. Bake in centre of oven for 45 minutes. Remove foil from roll.
6. Cut tomatoes in halves, place in tin and sprinkle with salt and pepper. Return tin to oven and cook for a further 15 minutes.
7. Place meat on a warmed serving dish, arrange some onions and tomatoes around, and place remainder in a warmed dish. Garnish meat dish with sprigs of parsley. Serve with cabbage.

CAULIFLOWER MEAT PIE
(recipe on page 39)

ITALIAN MEAT ROLL
(recipe on page 39)

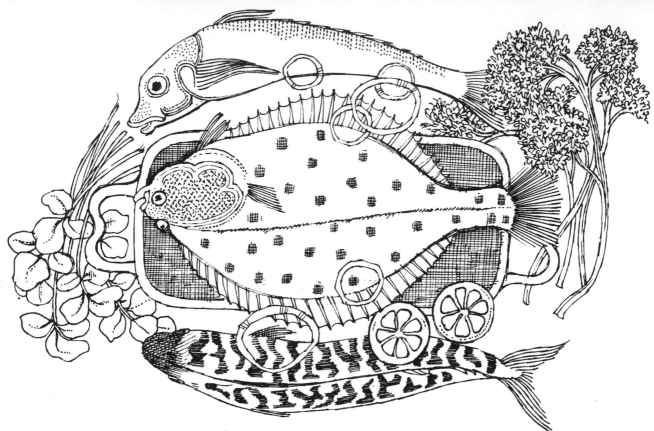

Savoury Fish Bake ✳

For 4 portions:

IMPERIAL	METRIC
4 tomatoes	4 tomatoes
1 large (13oz) carton frozen haddock fillets	1 large (370g) carton frozen haddock fillets
½ pint milk and water, mixed	250ml milk and water, mixed
1 small (¼lb) pack frozen peas	1 small (113g) pack frozen peas
4oz Cheddar cheese	100g Cheddar cheese
2 eggs	2 eggs
½ level teaspoon salt	1 x 2.5ml spoon salt
Pepper	Pepper

1. Prepare a moderate oven (190 deg C, 375 deg F, Gas Mark 5). Cut tomatoes in halves, place in a shallow ovenproof dish and cover with foil.
2. Place fish in a frying pan, with milk and water; cook until tender. Drain and reserve 4 x 15ml spoons (4 tablespoons) of fish liquor. Cook peas, as directed on pack. Grate cheese. Beat eggs, salt and a shake of pepper together in a small bowl.
3. Flake fish, removing skin, if necessary. Place in a bowl with the reserved liquor, peas, 75g (3oz) grated cheese and eggs. Mix together with a fork. Pour into a 600ml (1-pint) ovenproof dish and sprinkle with remaining grated cheese.
4. Place dish in top position of oven; place tomatoes in centre of oven. Bake for 30 minutes. Serve with a green salad, if desired.

Savoury Haddock Grill ✳

For 4 portions:

IMPERIAL	METRIC
1½lb haddock fillet	¾kg haddock fillet
4 rashers streaky bacon	4 rashers streaky bacon
2 tomatoes	2 tomatoes
Salt and pepper	Salt and pepper
4oz Cheshire cheese	100g Cheshire cheese

1. Wash fish, dry on kitchen paper and cut into 4 portions. Place in grill pan.
2. Prepare a moderate grill. Remove rind and bone from bacon; press rashers flat with a knife, to stretch rashers. Place grill rack in pan over fish; arrange bacon on rack.
3. Grill bacon for about 8 minutes, turning once, until lightly cooked, but not brown or crisp. Remove grill pan and roll up each rasher of bacon loosely, to make a curl; keep warm. Cut tomatoes in halves, sprinkle with a little salt and pepper; place in grill pan. Return pan to grill; continue cooking fish under tomatoes for about 5 minutes, depending on thickness of fish.
4. Remove from heat. Grate cheese. Top each fillet with a shake of pepper and some grated cheese. Return grill pan to heat and cook for 2 minutes, to melt the cheese.
5. Top each fillet with a bacon curl. Serve grill immediately with green beans.

Grilled Mackerel ✳

For 2 portions:

IMPERIAL	METRIC
1 large mackerel	1 large mackerel
1 teaspoon soy sauce	1 x 5ml spoon soy sauce
2 medium-sized tomatoes	2 medium-sized tomatoes
2 starch-reduced crispbreads	2 starch-reduced crispbreads
Low-fat spread (optional)	Low-fat spread (optional)
Watercress, to garnish	Watercress, to garnish

1. Cut head off mackerel, using a sharp knife. Cut along underside of fish, from head to tail. Scrape away any gut and blood vessels and discard. Wash under cold water and drain on kitchen paper.

2. Open fish and place, skin side uppermost, on a board. Press firmly along back of fish, to loosen backbone. Turn fish over and ease away backbone, starting at head end, cutting at tail end, to leave tail intact. Cut off fins.

3. Prepare a moderately hot grill; remove grill pan. Place mackerel, skin side downwards, on rack in grill pan. Sprinkle evenly with soy sauce. Cut tomatoes in halves and place on grill rack. Grill for about 10 minutes, until cooked. Place tomatoes on a warmed serving plate; keep hot.

4. Place crispbreads between 2 sheets of greaseproof paper; crush finely with a rolling pin. When fish is cooked, sprinkle crumbs over evenly; return fish to grill for 1 minute. Place fish on serving plate with tomatoes. Dot with a little low-fat spread, if desired; garnish with watercress. Serve immediately.

Fluffy Italian Plaice ✳

For 4 portions:

IMPERIAL	METRIC
4 plaice fillets	4 plaice fillets
Tomato ketchup	Tomato ketchup
¼ level teaspoon basil	½ x 2.5ml spoon basil
Salt and pepper	Salt and pepper
Half a medium-sized lemon	Half a medium-sized lemon
2 (6oz) cartons frozen whole leaf spinach	2 (170g) cartons frozen whole leaf spinach
1 egg	1 egg
4 level tablespoons low-calorie vinegar and oil dressing	4 x 15ml spoons low-calorie vinegar and oil dressing
1 level tablespoon chopped parsley	1 x 15ml spoon chopped parsley

1. Prepare a moderate grill. Remove rack from grill pan. Warm a shallow, ½-litre (1-pint) ovenproof serving dish.

2. Wash plaice fillets and remove skin. Place fillets, skinned side uppermost, on a board. Spread each with tomato ketchup; sprinkle with basil and a shake of salt and pepper. Roll up each fillet from the tail end.

3. Place fillets in grill pan. Squeeze juice from lemon. Sprinkle half lemon juice over fish; grill for 10 to 12 minutes, turning once and sprinkling with remaining lemon juice.

4. Cook spinach as directed on carton; drain well. Season with a little salt and pepper and turn out into ovenproof dish. Arrange plaice fillets on spinach; keep warm under grill.

5. Separate egg. Place yolk in a basin with vinegar and oil dressing and chopped parsley; mix well. Place white in a clean, grease-free bowl; whisk until stiff, then fold into egg-yolk mixture, using a metal spoon, until all egg white has been incorporated.

6. Pile dressing over fillets and spinach. Grill until golden brown. Serve immediately.

Balkan Fish Pie

For 4 portions:

IMPERIAL	METRIC
4oz cracker biscuits	100g cracker biscuits
2oz margarine	50g margarine
6oz Cheddar cheese	150g Cheddar cheese
10oz to 12oz cod fillet	250g to 300g cod fillet
1 egg	1 egg
1 (5.3oz) carton natural low-fat yoghourt	1 (150g) carton natural low-fat yoghourt
Salt and pepper	Salt and pepper
Sprig of parsley to garnish	Sprig of parsley to garnish

1. Prepare a moderate oven (190 deg C, 375 deg F, Gas Mark 5). Grease an 21cm (8½in) ovenglass pie plate.

2. Place biscuits in a paper bag and crush with the hands. Melt margarine in a small saucepan. Remove from heat and stir in crushed biscuits. Press on to base and sides of pie plate.

3. Cut cheese into 1cm (½in) cubes. Wash cod and remove skin; cut into 2cm (1in) cubes. Mix cheese and cod together and turn into pie plate.

4. Beat together egg, yoghourt and some salt and pepper; pour over fish mixture.

5. Place on a baking sheet and bake in centre of oven for 40 minutes, until set and golden and fish is tender. Garnish with a sprig of parsley. Serve hot with a green salad.

(ABOVE LEFT)
LAMB CHOPS PROVENCE
(recipe on page 46)

(BELOW LEFT)
SLIMMERS' OMELET STACK
(recipe on page 46)

(ABOVE RIGHT)
CELERY-STUFFED ROAST LAMB
SNOWY ORANGE PUDDING
(recipes, pages 46 and 63)

(BELOW RIGHT)
GLAZED GRILLED CHICKEN
(recipe on page 47)

Lamb Chops Provence *

(pictured on page 44)

For 4 portions:

IMPERIAL	METRIC
4 lamb chump chops	4 lamb chump chops
2 medium-sized onions	2 medium-sized onions
½lb courgettes	¼kg courgettes
1 medium-sized green pepper	1 medium-sized green pepper
½lb tomatoes	¼kg tomatoes
1 level teaspoon salt	1 x 5ml spoon salt
Pepper	Pepper
Pinch of mixed dried herbs	Pinch of mixed dried herbs

1. Prepare a moderate oven (190 deg C, 375 deg F, Gas Mark 5).
2. Trim fat from chops. Peel and slice onions. Wash courgettes; cut into 1cm (½in) slices. Wash green pepper; cut into thin rings, discarding seeds, core and white pith. Place tomatoes in a bowl; cover with boiling water. Leave for 1 minute; drain, peel and slice.
3. Arrange vegetables in a shallow, ovenproof dish; sprinkle with salt, a shake of pepper and herbs.
4. Arrange chops on vegetables; cover with a lid or foil. Cook in centre of oven for 1 to 1¼ hours. Serve with green beans and new potatoes.
NOTE: In place of courgettes, ¼kg (½lb) marrow, cut into 1cm (½in) cubes, may be used.

Slimmers' Omelet Stack *

(pictured on page 44)

For 4 portions:

IMPERIAL	METRIC
FILLINGS	FILLINGS
4 small tomatoes	4 small tomatoes
2oz button mushrooms	50g button mushrooms
4oz cooked peas	100g cooked peas
4oz cottage cheese with chives	100g cottage cheese with chives

OMELETS	OMELETS
8 eggs	8 eggs
Salt	Salt
Oil	Oil
A little Farmhouse Cheddar cheese, grated	A litte Farmhouse Cheddar cheese, grated

1. Prepare a moderately hot grill; heat oven at lowest setting.
2. Thinly slice tomatoes; reserve 7 slices for garnish and chop remainder. Wash mushrooms, dry on kitchen paper and thinly slice.
3. To make omelets: Break 2 eggs into a small basin. Add ½ x 2.5ml spoon (¼ level teaspoon) salt and beat with a fork, until just mixed; add one of the 4 fillings. Repeat with remaining eggs and fillings. Heat a little oil slowly in a small, 15cm (6in) omelet or frying pan; swirl, to coat pan, then pour in egg mixture from one basin. Cook slowly until underside is golden brown and edge is set.
4. Grill for 2 to 3 minutes, until the top of the omelet is set.
5. Slide omelet on to a warmed serving dish; place in oven, to keep warm. Make 3 more omelets in same way; pile on top of one another on serving dish, to form a 'cake'.
6. Arrange reserved tomato slices, in a circle, on top of omelets and top with grated cheese. Grill for 3 to 4 minutes, until cheese begins to melt.
7. Serve immediately, with green salad and starch-reduced rolls or one new potato per portion.

Celery-stuffed Roast Lamb *

(pictured on page 45)

For 4 portions:

IMPERIAL	METRIC
1½lb best end neck of lamb	¾kg best end neck of lamb
1lb carrots	½kg carrots
Boiling water	Boiling water
Salt	Salt

STUFFING	STUFFING
2 sticks of celery	2 sticks of celery
2oz cottage cheese	50g cottage cheese
2 level teaspoons chopped parsley	1 x 10ml spoon chopped parsley
Pepper	Pepper

4 medium-sized potatoes	4 medium-sized potatoes
Oil	Oil
1 level tablespoon cornflour	1 x 15ml spoon cornflour
Gravy browning	Gravy browning

1. Bone meat or ask your butcher to do this for you. Trim off excess fat from meat. Place bones in a saucepan, cover with water and simmer for 1 hour. Strain 250ml (½ pint) stock into a measuring jug; reserve.
2. Peel and thinly slice carrots. Place in a 1¼-litre (2-pint) ovenproof dish; cover with boiling water. Add 1 x 10ml spoon (1 rounded teaspoon) salt and cover dish with a lid or foil.
3. Prepare a moderate oven (190 deg C, 375 deg F, Gas Mark 5). Place a rack in a small roasting tin.
4. Wash and chop celery. Mix together cheese, celery, parsley, 1 x 2.5ml spoon (½ level teaspoon) salt and a shake of pepper.

5. Place meat on a board, boned side uppermost. Spread stuffing evenly over meat; roll up meat firmly. Tie into 4 sections with string.

6. Place meat on rack. Wash and peel potatoes; cut into even-sized pieces. Cook in boiling, salted water for 3 minutes. Drain and arrange around meat on rack; brush with oil.

7. Place on shelf just above centre of oven; cook for $1\frac{1}{2}$ to $1\frac{3}{4}$ hours. Place carrots on shelf just below centre of oven; cook for $1\frac{1}{4}$ hours, until tender.

8. Remove string from meat. Place meat on a warmed serving dish and potatoes in a warmed dish; keep hot. Pour off fat from tin. Stir in cornflour; gradually blend in 250ml ($\frac{1}{2}$ pint) reserved stock and a few drops gravy browning. Bring to boil, stirring, and cook for 2 minutes. Taste and season with salt and pepper. Pour into a warmed gravy boat. Serve lamb with drained carrots, Sugar-free Mint Sauce (see recipe) and Brussels sprouts. Serve roast potatoes and gravy for the non-slimmers.

Sugar-free Mint Sauce ✱

IMPERIAL	METRIC
1 teacupful mint leaves	1 teacupful mint leaves
2 tablespoons boiling water	2 x 15ml spoons boiling water
3 sugar substitute tablets or liquid sweetener	3 sugar substitute tablets or liquid sweetener
4 tablespoons vinegar	4 x 15ml spoons vinegar

Wash and finely chop mint leaves. Place in a small basin, add boiling water and sugar substitute tablets, if used; stir well. Add vinegar; sweeten to taste with liquid sweetener, if used. Place in a sauce boat. Serve with lamb or use as a salad dressing.

Glazed Grilled Chicken ✱

(pictured on page 45)

For 4 portions:

IMPERIAL	METRIC
4 chicken joints	4 chicken joints
2 level tablespoons low-calorie vinegar and oil dressing	2 x 15ml spoons low-calorie vinegar and oil dressing
1 tablespoon bottled pure lemon juice	1 x 15ml spoon bottled pure lemon juice
Paprika	Paprika
Carrots and watercress to garnish	Carrots and watercress to garnish

1. Prepare a moderate grill. Place chicken joints in grill pan; cook for 25 to 30 minutes, turning once.

2. Place joints on a board. Using a piece of kitchen paper, firmly hold skin of chicken and pull away from flesh; discard skin. Arrange joints on a warmed serving dish; place under grill, to keep warm.

3. Place vinegar and oil dressing and lemon juice in a basin; mix well. Spoon dressing evenly over chicken joints; sprinkle a little paprika over surface. Garnish with carrots and watercress. Serve with more carrots and a green salad.

Piquant Cod ✱

For 4 portions:

IMPERIAL	METRIC
2 large onions	2 large onions
1oz margarine	25g margarine
1 (14oz) carton 4 frozen cod steaks, just thawed	1 (396g) carton 4 frozen cod steaks, just thawed
Salt and pepper	Salt and pepper
Mixed dried herbs	Mixed dried herbs
2 tablespoons vinegar	2 x 15ml spoons vinegar
3 drops liquid sweetener	3 drops liquid sweetener
1 small (8oz) can tomatoes	1 small (226g) can tomatoes

1. Prepare a moderate oven (190 dcg C, 375 deg F, Gas Mark 5).

2. Peel onions; slice in rings. Melt margarine in a small saucepan and fry onion until golden brown. Place cod steaks in an ovenproof serving dish; sprinkle with some salt and pepper and a pinch of mixed dried herbs. Top with onions.

3. Stir vinegar and liquid sweetener into tomatoes and pour around cod steaks; cover and cook in centre of oven for 40 minutes.

LIVER-FILLED ONIONS
(recipe on page 50)

Liver-filled Onions

(pictured on pages 48, 49)

For 4 portions:

IMPERIAL	METRIC
4 large onions	4 large onions
1oz cooking fat	25g cooking fat
8oz ox liver	¼kg ox liver
1 level teaspoon salt	1 x 5ml spoon salt
Pepper	Pepper
1 small (8oz) can tomatoes	1 small (226g) can tomatoes
8 rashers streaky bacon	8 rashers streaky bacon

1. Peel onions, keeping them whole. Cook in boiling, salted water for 30 to 40 minutes, depending on size, until tender, but not soft. Drain and cool. Carefully cut a thin slice from top of each onion and, using a small, sharp knife, cut out inside of each onion leaving a wall of onion 2 layers thick. Place onion shells in a shallow, ovenproof dish. Roughly chop inside of onions.

2. Prepare a moderate oven (190 deg C, 375 deg F, Gas Mark 5).

3. Melt cooking fat in a frying pan and quickly fry liver until firm, but not hard; remove from pan. Fry chopped onion until deep golden brown. Mince liver and onion together or chop very finely. Mix in salt and a shake of pepper.

4. Pile liver mixture into onion shells. Place contents of can of tomatoes in a basin and mash with a fork; mix in any remaining liver mixture. Spoon over and around onions; cover with a piece of greased greaseproof paper. Cook in centre of oven for 20 minutes; after 10 minutes, remove paper and baste onions with tomato sauce; replace paper.

5. Remove rind and bone from bacon. Press rashers flat with the back of a knife, to stretch rashers, then cut across in halves. Roll up each piece of bacon.

6. Remove paper from onions and baste with sauce. Place a bacon roll on each onion and remaining rolls, join sides downwards, in a small tin on shelf below onions. Cook for a further 15 to 20 minutes, until bacon rolls are golden brown.

7. Arrange onions on a dish with bacon rolls and serve hot with a green vegetable.

Mackerel Bake ✳

For 2 portions:

IMPERIAL	METRIC
1 large mackerel	1 large mackerel
2oz mushrooms	50g mushrooms
1 large tomato	1 large tomato
Salt and pepper	Salt and pepper
¼ level teaspoon mixed dried herbs	½ x 2.5ml spoon mixed dried herbs
1 teaspoon lemon juice	1 x 5ml spoon lemon juice

1. Prepare a moderate oven (190 deg C, 375 deg F, Gas Mark 4).

2. Remove head and fins from mackerel, using a sharp knife. Cut along underside of mackerel, from head to tail. Scrape away any gut and blood vessels and discard. Wash under cold water and dry on kitchen paper. Place mackerel on a large piece of foil on a baking sheet.

3. Wash and slice mushrooms; cut tomato into 6 slices. Sprinkle a little salt, pepper and herbs inside fish. Place mushrooms and tomato over fish. Sprinkle with a little salt and lemon juice.

4. Bring foil over fish and fold edges together, to make a parcel. Place in centre of oven and bake for 25 minutes. Serve with peas.

Mustard Cod Grill ✳

For 4 portions:

IMPERIAL	METRIC
4oz button mushrooms	100g button mushrooms
1 medium-sized lemon	1 medium-sized lemon
1½lb cod fillet	¾kg cod fillet
Made mustard	Made mustard
Salt and pepper	Salt and pepper

1. Prepare a moderately hot grill. Remove rack from grill pan.

2. Wash mushrooms; cut in halves and place in grill pan. Grate rind and squeeze juice from half the lemon; cut remaining half lemon into 4 wedges.

3. Wash fish; dry on kitchen paper. Cut into 4 portions; spread each portion with a little made mustard and place in grill pan. Sprinkle fish with a little salt and pepper, lemon rind and juice.

4. Grill fish and mushrooms for about 8 minutes, depending on thickness of fish. Stir mushrooms occasionally and baste fish, to keep moist. Serve immediately with lemon wedges, carrots and broccoli.

Yogi Tomato Salad

For 4 portions:

IMPERIAL	METRIC
2 sticks of celery	2 sticks of celery
6oz Cheddar cheese	150g Cheddar cheese
1oz walnuts	25g walnuts
1 (5.3oz) carton natural low-fat yoghourt	1 (150ml) carton natural low-fat yoghourt
1 rounded teaspoon chopped parsley	1 x 10ml spoon chopped parsley
Salt and pepper	Salt and pepper
1lb tomatoes	½kg tomatoes
Lettuce	Lettuce
Watercress	Watercress

1. Wash, trim and finely chop celery. Finely grate cheese. Chop walnuts.

2. Place yoghourt in a bowl and add celery, cheese, walnuts, parsley and some salt and pepper. Mix well together.

3. Wash tomatoes and cut in halves; arrange on bed of lettuce and sprinkle with salt. Divide cheese mixture between tomatoes and pile on top of each. Garnish each with a small sprig of watercress.

Shrimp Salad *

For 2 portions:

IMPERIAL	METRIC
1 medium-sized carrot	1 medium-sized carrot
1 stick of celery	1 stick of celery
Quarter of a medium-sized green pepper	Quarter of a medium-sized green pepper
½ teaspoon lemon juice	1 x 2.5ml spoon lemon juice
2 level tablespoons low-calorie vinegar and oil dressing	2 x 15ml spoons low-calorie vinegar and oil dressing
Salt and pepper	Salt and pepper
1 (7¼oz) can shrimps	1 (205g) can shrimps
Lettuce leaves	Lettuce leaves
Tomato wedges	Tomato wedges
Cucumber slices	Cucumber slices
Lemon wedges (optional)	Lemon wedges (optional)

1. Peel carrot and wash celery. Cut carrot, celery and pepper into small dice. Place in a bowl with lemon juice, vinegar and oil dressing and a shake each of salt and pepper.

2. Drain shrimps; add to bowl and stir lightly. Arrange a few lettuce leaves on 2 individual serving plates; divide shrimp mixture between plates. Garnish with a few tomato wedges, cucumber slices and lemon wedges, if desired.

NOTE: Alternatively, use canned tuna. For a packed lunch, place shredded lettuce in a plastic container with a lid and top with shrimp mixture, tomato wedges and cucumber slices.

Slimmers' Egg Savoury *

For 4 portions:

IMPERIAL	METRIC
8 eggs	8 eggs
1 lettuce	1 lettuce
4 tomatoes	4 tomatoes
8 tablespoons evaporated milk	125ml evaporated milk
3 tablespoons lemon juice	3 x 15ml spoons lemon juice
2 gherkins	2 gherkins
½ level teaspoon made mustard	1 x 2.5ml spoon made mustard
2 teaspoons vinegar	1 x 10ml spoon vinegar
Salt and pepper	Salt and pepper
Pinch of paprika	Pinch of paprika

1. Hard boil eggs for 10 minutes; crack and leave to cool in cold water. Shell and dry on kitchen paper.

2. Slice hard-boiled eggs. Remove and discard outer leaves from lettuce. Wash lettuce and dry well. Cut each tomato into 8 wedges.

3. Place evaporated milk in a basin; add lemon juice and mix well. Thinly slice gherkins and add to mixture with mustard, vinegar and a little salt and pepper.

4. Divide lettuce leaves between 4 plates; arrange 2 sliced hard-boiled eggs on each plate, sprinkle with salt. Top each with dressing. Sprinkle with paprika and arrange tomato wedges around the edge of each plate.

(BELOW) RAINBOW SALAD
(recipe on page 54)

(OPPOSITE) TUSCANY SALAD
(recipe on page 54)

Tuscany Salad

(pictured on page 53)

For 4 portions:

IMPERIAL	METRIC
Salt	Salt
½lb cod fillet	¼kg cod fillet
2 eggs	2 eggs
1 (7oz) can tuna steak	1 (198g) can tuna steak
2 level tablespoons low-calorie vinegar and oil dressing	2 x 15ml spoons low-calorie vinegar and oil dressing
2 teaspoons lemon juice	1 x 10ml spoon lemon juice
½lb tomatoes	¼kg tomatoes
Half a green pepper	Half a green pepper
1 lettuce	1 lettuce
1 (2oz) can anchovy fillets	1 (56g) can anchovy fillets
5 black olives	5 black olives

1. Bring about 2.5cm (1in) water to the boil in a saucepan; add a little salt and the cod fillet. Reduce heat, cover and cook very gently until cod is tender, about 8 minutes; drain. Remove skin and any bones; flake fish.

2. Hard boil eggs for 10 minutes, crack and leave to cool in cold water. Shell and dry on kitchen paper. Cut into quarters lengthwise.

3. Drain and flake tuna. Place dressing and lemon juice in a basin. Add cod, tuna and eggs; mix together lightly.

4. Place tomatoes in a bowl and cover with boiling water. Leave for 1 minute; drain, then peel and cut into slices. Wash and thinly slice green pepper. Remove and discard outer leaves from lettuce; wash lettuce and drain well. Reserve inside leaves and finely shred remainder.

5. Arrange whole lettuce leaves around edge of a serving dish. Mix tomatoes, green pepper and shredded lettuce together. Arrange in centre of dish. Pile fish and egg mixture on top.

6. Drain anchovy fillets; cut in halves lengthwise. Cut olives in halves; remove stones. Arrange anchovies in a lattice pattern over fish mixture; arrange olive halves in some 'squares'. Serve salad with starch-reduced rolls.

Rainbow Salad ✳

(pictured on page 52)

For 4 portions:

IMPERIAL	METRIC
4oz cooked ham	100g cooked ham
8oz cottage cheese	200g cottage cheese
Pinch of Cayenne pepper	Pinch of Cayenne pepper
¼ level teaspoon salt	½ x 2.5ml spoon salt
2 eggs	2 eggs
Half a cucumber	Half a cucumber
4 sticks of celery	4 sticks of celery
2 medium-sized carrots	2 medium-sized carrots
4 large lettuce leaves	4 large lettuce leaves
2 red-skinned eating apples	2 red-skinned eating apples
1 tablespoon lemon juice	1 x 15ml spoon lemon juice
Sprig of parsley	Sprig of parsley

DRESSING	DRESSING
1 (5.3oz) carton natural low-fat yoghourt	1 (150ml) carton natural low-fat yoghourt
1 teaspoon lemon juice	1 x 5ml spoon lemon juice
Pinch of garlic salt (optional)	Pinch of garlic salt (optional)
1 level teaspoon made mustard	1 x 5ml spoon made mustard
Pepper	Pepper
Paprika	Paprika

1. Cut ham into small dice; place in a bowl with cottage cheese, Cayenne pepper and salt. Mix well with a fork.

2. Hard boil eggs for 10 minutes; crack and leave to cool in cold water. Shell and dry on kitchen paper.

3. Cut thin slices of cucumber and arrange around edge of a large, flat serving dish. Cut remaining cucumber into small dice. Wash and chop celery. Wash, scrape and grate carrots. Wash lettuce. Wash, core and chop apples.

4. Place diced cucumber, celery, apples, carrots, and 1 x 15ml spoon (1 tablespoon) lemon juice in a bowl. Mix well together; arrange on serving dish.

5. Arrange lettuce leaves in centre of apple and celery mixture and pile the cottage cheese mixture on top.

6. Cut hard-boiled eggs in halves lengthwise; place in centre of cottage cheese mixture. Place a sprig of parsley in centre.

7. Mix yoghourt, lemon juice, garlic salt, if used, mustard and a shake of pepper together in a basin, sprinkle with paprika and serve with the salad.

DESSERTS

Orange Dream Cups *

(pictured opposite and on front cover)

For 8 portions:

IMPERIAL	METRIC
3 large oranges	3 large oranges
2 egg whites	2 egg whites
3 (5.3 oz) cartons fat-free yoghourt	3 (150ml) cartons fat-free yoghourt
Liquid sweetener	Liquid sweetener
Toasted flake almonds (optional)	Toasted flake almonds (optional)

1. Scrub oranges. Using a sharp knife or potato peeler, pare several long pieces of rind from 1 orange, taking care not to include any white pith, and reserve. Finely grate 1 x 5ml spoon (1 teaspoon) rind from another orange.

2. Using a sharp or serrated knife, cut remaining peel from all oranges, including white pith. Hold each orange over a basin, to catch juice, and cut out segments of orange. Place in basin; cut segments in halves. Divide orange segments and juice equally between 8 small serving glasses.

3. Place egg whites in a clean, grease-free basin and whisk until stiff, but not dry. Drain any liquid off top of yoghourt; add yoghourt and grated orange rind to egg whites. Whisk slowly until thoroughly mixed, adding a few drops of liquid sweetener to taste. Divide mixture equally between glasses.

4. Cut reserved pieces of orange rind into long, narrow strips; chop almonds roughly, if used. Decorate top of each Dream Cup with a few chopped almonds and a strip of orange rind; chill. Serve with thin wafers, if desired.

Raspberry Petal Dessert *

For 8 portions:

IMPERIAL	METRIC
Half a medium-sized lemon	Half a medium-sized lemon
4 medium-sized dessert pears	4 medium-sized dessert pears
¾lb frozen raspberries	300g frozen raspberries
1oz (or 2 envelopes) gelatine	25g (or 2 envelopes) gelatine
Liquid sweetener	Liquid sweetener

1. Squeeze juice from lemon and place in a large saucepan. Peel pears; cut in halves lengthwise and carefully remove cores. Place in saucepan; add sufficient water to just cover pears. Bring to boil, reduce heat, cover and simmer for 10 minutes until pears are just tender. Carefully remove pears from pan, using a draining spoon. Place on a wire rack to drain and leave liquid in pan to cool. When pears are cold, chill in refrigerator.

2. If necessary, make up liquid in pan to 625ml (1¼ pints) with water. Add 150g (6oz) raspberries,

bring to boil and cook for 3 to 4 minutes, until fruit is pulpy, pressing raspberries with back of a wooden spoon to release juice. Strain contents of pan through a nylon sieve into a large bowl; cool.

3. Measure 6 x 15ml spoons (6 tablespoons) water into a small basin; add gelatine and stir. Place basin in a pan of water over a moderate heat and stir until gelatine has dissolved. Stir gelatine into strained raspberry liquid and sweeten to taste with liquid sweetener. Reserve 125ml (¼ pint) raspberry liquid and leave to cool, but not set. Chill remaining liquid until on the point of setting.

4. Using a rotary beater or electric whisk, whisk the chilled mixture until light anf foamy. Reserve 75g (3oz) raspberries for decoration and fold remaining fruit into whisked mixture. Turn into a round, 22.5cm (9in) 1½ litre (3-pint) glass serving bowl; level top and chill until set.

5. When set, arrange chilled pear halves in a petal design on top of jelly. Spoon reserved raspberry liquid over pears, to glaze and form a layer of clear raspberry jelly on top of whisked jelly; chill until set. To decorate: Place 1 reserved raspberry between each pear half and pile remainder in centre. Serve chilled with Kirsch Dessert Topping (see Whisked Dessert Topping below).

Whisked Dessert Topping *

For 6 to 8 portions:

IMPERIAL	METRIC
1 level teaspoon gelatine	1 x 5ml spoon gelatine
2 rounded tablespoons dried skimmed milk	4 x 15ml spoon dried skimmed milk
4 drops vanilla essence	4 drops vanilla essence
Liquid sweetener	Liquid sweetener

1. Measure 1 tablespoon cold water into a small basin; add gelatine and stir. Place basin in a pan of water over a moderate heat; stir until gelatine has dissolved.

2. Place dried milk in a measuring jug; make up to 100ml (4 fluid oz) with water. Stir in gelatine and vanilla essence; pour into a basin and leave in refrigerator, until just on the point of setting.

3. Using an electric whisk or rotary beater, whisk until mixture is thick and fluffy. Add a few drops of liquid sweetener, to taste, and continue whisking until mixture is very white and has doubled in volume. Chill for 5 minutes in refrigerator before piling into a serving bowl. Serve with cold desserts, Fruit-flavour Jelly (see recipe on page 58) and stewed fruit.

NOTE: For a Kirsch-flavour topping, omit vanilla essence and whisk 1 x 5ml spoon (1 teaspoon) Kirsch and a few drops of lemon juice into gelatine mixture, when on the point of setting.

RASPBERRY PETAL DESSERT
KIRSCH DESSERT TOPPING
(a variation of Whisked
Dessert Topping)
ORANGE DREAM CUPS

Quick 'Cream' *

For 4 portions:

IMPERIAL	METRIC
4 rounded tablespoons dried skimmed milk	8 x 15ml spoons dried skimmed milk
Vanilla essence (optional)	Vanilla essence (optional)

1. Place dried skimmed milk in a small basin. Add 3 or 4 x 15ml spoons (3 to 4 tablespoons) cold water and beat well until smooth.
2. Add a few drops of vanilla essence, if desired. Serve with hot and cold desserts or whisk into Fruit-flavour Jelly (see recipe).

Apple Fool *

For 4 portions:

IMPERIAL	METRIC
1 level teaspoon gelatine	1 x 5ml spoon gelatine
4 rounded tablespoons dried skimmed milk	125ml dried skimmed milk
4 drops vanilla essence	4 drops vanilla essence
1 lb cooking apples	½kg cooking apples
Liquid sweetener	Liquid sweetener
Green or red food colouring (optional)	Green or red food colouring (optional)

1. Measure 1 x 15ml spoon (1 tablespoon) cold water into a small basin; add gelatine and stir. Place basin in a pan of water over a moderate heat; stir until gelatine has dissolved.
2. Place dried skimmed milk in a measuring jug and make up to 125ml (4 fluid oz) with water; beat until smooth. Stir in dissolved gelatine and vanilla essence. Place in refrigerator or leave in a cool place until just on the point of setting.
3. Peel, core and thinly slice apples. Place in a medium-sized saucepan with 4 tablespoons water; bring to boil, reduce heat, cover and cook for 5 to 6 minutes, stirring occasionally, until apple is tender. Remove from heat; beat until smooth using wooden spoon. Leave to cool; chill thoroughly.
4. Using an electric whisk or rotary beater, whisk the skimmed milk mixture until thick, very white, fluffy and almost doubled in volume. Whisk in 3 or 4 drops of liquid sweetener and a few drops of food colouring, if desired.
5. Fold whisked skimmed milk mixture into the chilled apple, using a metal spoon, until all whisked mixture has been incorporated. Turn out into a chilled serving dish and serve immediately.
NOTE: If made in advance, make up to end of step 4. Just before serving, lightly whisk milk mixture once more, then fold into chilled apple.

Fruit-flavour Jelly *

For 4 portions:

IMPERIAL	METRIC
1 level tablespoon gelatine	1 x 15ml spoon gelatine
6 fluid oz low-calorie fruit drink (orange, lemon or lime)	150ml low-calorie fruit drink (orange, lemon or lime)

1. Measure 3 x 15ml spoons (3 tablespoons) cold water into a small basin; add gelatine and stir. Place basin in a pan of water over a moderate heat; stir until gelatine has dissolved.
2. Measure low-calorie drink into a measuring jug, add dissolved gelatine and make up to 500ml (1 pint) with water. Pour into a serving dish; leave in a cool place until set. Serve jelly by itself or with Quick 'Cream' and fresh fruit.
NOTE: If desired, set fresh fruit in jelly, or whisk jelly, when on point of setting, until foamy. Alternatively, for a creamy mixture, add a little Quick 'Cream' to jelly before whisking, or fold into whisked jelly.

Nell Gwynne Jellies

For 4 portions:

IMPERIAL	METRIC
1 (11oz) can mandarin oranges	1 (312g) can mandarin oranges
1 orange or tangerine flavour jelly	1 orange or tangerine flavour jelly
1 egg	1 egg
1 Swiss roll	1 Swiss roll
Angelica 'leaves'	Angelica 'leaves'

1. Strain syrup from oranges and place in a small saucepan. Add jelly cubes and heat gently, stirring occasionally, until jelly has melted.
2. Beat egg and add to jelly. Stir continuously with a wooden spoon until mixture just boils; remove from heat.
3. Strain into a measuring jug and make up to 500ml (1 pint) with cold water.
4. Pour into 4 individual jelly moulds or small teacups and leave to set.
5. To serve family portion: Cut Swiss roll into 9 slices and place 3 slices on each of 3 small plates. Unmould 1 jelly on to each plate and surround with some of the mandarin oranges. Decorate with angelica 'leaves'. To serve slimmer's portion: Unmould a jelly on to a small plate and surround with remaining mandarin oranges and angelica 'leaves'.
NOTE: This serves 1 slimmer's portion and 3 family portions.

Melon Bowl Fruit Salad *

For 6 portions:

IMPERIAL	METRIC
Half a honeydew melon	Half a honeydew melon
1 medium-sized orange	1 medium-sized orange
4oz grapes	100g grapes
1 red-skinned eating apple	1 red-skinned eating apple
2 tablespoons less-sharp bottled pure lemon juice	2 x 15ml spoons less-sharp bottled pure lemon juice
2 apricots	2 apricots
4oz fresh strawberries	100g fresh strawberries

1. Scoop out melon seeds and discard. Cut out balls of melon, using a special gadget or a small teaspoon. Place in a bowl; reserve melon shell.
2. Using a sharp or serrated knife, cut peel from orange, including white pith. Hold orange over bowl containing melon, to catch juice, and cut out segments of orange, discarding pith and pips; place in bowl.
3. Using a sterilised hair grip, insert rounded end into each grape and pull out pips, one at a time. (Alternatively, cut grapes in halves and remove pips.) Wash grapes and dry on kitchen paper, before adding to bowl. Wash apple; cut into quarters. Remove core; cut apple into small pieces. Place in a basin, add lemon juice and stir lightly, to coat.
4. Place apricots in a bowl; cover with boiling water. Leave for 1 minute; drain, remove skins and cut into quarters, removing stones. Add to other fruits in bowl.
5. Hull and wash strawberries; dry on kitchen paper. Cut in halves, if large; add to bowl. Stir gently and leave bowl in a cool place until ready to serve.
6. To serve: Stir apple and lemon juice into bowl; pile mixture into melon shell. Fill a shallow glass bowl with ice cubes; place fruit-filled melon on top.

Stewed Apple *

For 4 portions:

IMPERIAL	METRIC
1lb cooking apples	½kg cooking apples
Liquid sweetener	Liquid sweetener

1. Peel, core and slice apples. Place in a medium-sized saucepan with 4 x 15ml spoons (4 tablespoons) water. Bring to boil, reduce heat, cover; simmer for 5 to 6 minutes, until apple is tender.
2. Leave to cool, if desired. Sweeten to taste with liquid sweetener.
3. Serve hot or cold, with low-fat or fat-free natural yoghourt, Quick 'Cream' or Whisked Dessert Topping (recipe on page 56), or egg custard; flavour with ground cinnamon, grated orange or lemon rind, or stir into Fruit-flavour Jelly (see recipe).

Orange Yoghourt Cups *

For 4 portions:

IMPERIAL	METRIC
4 medium-sized oranges	4 medium-sized oranges
2 rounded teaspoons gelatine	2 x 10ml spoons gelatine
1 small (5.3oz) carton natural low-fat yoghourt	1 small (150ml) carton natural low-fat yoghourt
Angelica 'leaves'	Angelica 'leaves'

1. Cut 2 oranges in halves and squeeze juice. Reserve orange halves and remove pith from centres with a spoon. Place 125ml ($\frac{1}{4}$ pint) orange juice in a small basin; add gelatine and stir. Place basin in a pan of water over a moderate heat; stir until gelatine has dissolved. Leave to cool slightly.
2. Using a sharp or serrated knife, cut peel from remaining oranges, including white pith. Hold each orange over a bowl, to catch juice; cut out segments of orange. Chop segments roughly and add juice to bowl.
3. Add yoghourt to bowl; stir in cooled orange juice and gelatine. Leave in a cool place until mixture has thickened and almost set; pile into prepared orange cups. Decorate with angelica 'leaves'.
NOTE: Omit angelica from slimmer's portion.

Coffee Mousse

For 6 portions:

IMPERIAL	METRIC
1 large can evaporated milk	1 large can evaporated milk
1 level tablespoon gelatine	1 x 15ml spoon gelatine
3 level dessertspoons instant coffee	2 x 15ml spoons instant coffee
8 sugar substitute tablets or liquid sweetener	8 sugar substitute tablets or liquid sweetener

1. Place can of evaporated milk in a medium-sized saucepan and cover with boiling water; boil for 15 minutes. Remove from saucepan and leave to cool for 5 minutes. Cover top of can with a cloth or treble thickness of kitchen paper, then open with a can opener.
2. Measure 3 x 15ml spoons (3 tablespoons) cold water into a small basin; add gelatine and stir. Place basin in a pan of water over a moderate heat; stir until gelatine has dissolved.
3. Place coffee and sugar substitute tablets, if used, in a large bowl. Add 2 x 15ml spoons (2 tablespoons) boiling water and stir until dissolved. Add gelatine and evaporated milk; stir well. Leave in a cool place until mixture is on the point of setting.
4. Whisk until mixture has doubled in volume; sweeten to taste with liquid sweetener, if used. Turn into a serving bowl; leave in a cool place until set.

Peach Sailboats *

For 4 portions:

IMPERIAL	METRIC
1 medium-sized orange	1 medium-sized orange
1 small (4oz) carton cottage cheese	1 small (113g) carton cottage cheese
Liquid sweetener	Liquid sweetener
2 ripe peaches	2 ripe peaches
Sprigs of mint	Sprigs of mint

1. Prepare a moderate oven (190 deg C, 375 deg F, Gas Mark 5).
2. Scrub orange. Cut 4 thin slices from centre; reserve for decoration. Squeeze juice from remainder of orange and reserve. Grate 1 x 2.5ml spoon (½ level teaspoon) rind from orange shells; place in a basin.
3. Add cottage cheese and 1 drop of liquid sweetener to orange rind; mix well.
4. Peel peaches. (If skins are difficult to remove, place peaches in a basin; cover with boiling water; drain and peel.) Cut peaches in halves; remove stones. Place peaches, cut sides uppermost, in a small, shallow ovenproof dish.
5. Divide cottage cheese mixture between hollows in peaches and pour orange juice over. Cover with foil and place in centre of oven; cook for 35 to 40 minutes, until peaches are tender.
6. Cut each slice of orange through to centre; twist and place one slice over cottage cheese on each piece. Decorate dish with small sprigs of mint before serving. Serve hot or cold.

NOTE: If not on reducing diet and if fresh peaches are not available, use canned peaches (thoroughly drain syrup and dry peaches on kitchen paper).

Apple Sorbet with Blackberries *

For 4 portions:

IMPERIAL	METRIC
½lb cooking apples	¼kg cooking apples
Liquid sweetener	Liquid sweetener
2 level teaspoons gelatine	1 x 10ml spoon gelatine
1 (5.3oz) carton natural yoghourt	1 (150g) carton natural yoghourt
Green food colouring	Green food colouring
1 egg white	1 egg white
½lb blackberries	¼kg blackberries

1. Turn refrigerator to coldest setting. Peel, core and slice apples. Place in a saucepan, with 2 x 15ml spoons (2 tablespoons) water. Cover, cook gently until apples are very soft. Sieve apples or liquidise in an electric blender; sweeten to taste with liquid sweetener.

PEACH SAILBOATS
APPLE SORBET WITH
BLACKBERRIES

2. Measure 2 x 15ml spoons (2 tablespoons) water into a small basin; add gelatine and stir. Place basin in a pan of water over a moderate heat and stir until gelatine has dissolved. Stir dissolved gelatine into apple purée. Leave until just on point of setting.
3. Whisk in yoghourt and a few drops of food colouring.
4. Whisk egg white until stiff, but not dry; fold into apple mixture, using a metal spoon.
5. Place mixture in a freezing tray or plastic tray and place in frozen-food compartment of refrigerator; leave until frozen. Turn refrigerator back to normal setting.
6. To serve: Cut sorbet into 2cm (¾in) cubes. Wash blackberries; dry on kitchen paper. Divide blackberries and sorbet between 4 individual glass dishes. Serve immediately.

Lemon Snow *

For 4 portions:

IMPERIAL	METRIC
1 medium-sized lemon	1 medium-sized lemon
1 level tablespoon gelatine	1 x 15ml spoon gelatine
12 sugar substitute tablets or liquid sweetener	12 sugar substitute tablets or liquid sweetener
1 egg white	1 egg white
Angelica 'leaves'	Angelica 'leaves'

1. Scrub lemon; using a sharp knife or potato peeler, cut peel from lemon, taking care not to include any white pith. Place peel in a saucepan with 250ml (½ pint) water. Bring to boil; remove from heat. Squeeze lemon juice and pour into a bowl.
2. Measure 3 x 15ml spoons (3 tablespoons) cold water into a small basin; add gelatine and stir. Place basin in a pan of water over a moderate heat; stir until gelatine has dissolved.
3. Strain lemon peel and water into lemon juice. Add gelatine and sugar substitute tablets; stir until dissolved. Alternatively, sweeten to taste with liquid sweetener. Leave in a cool place until mixture is almost set.
4. Add egg white and whisk until mixture has doubled in volume. Pour into 4 sundae glasses. Leave to set and decorate with angelica 'leaves'.

Orange Banana Delice

For 4 portions:

IMPERIAL	METRIC
4 large oranges	4 large oranges
2 bananas	2 bananas
1 rounded tablespoon castor sugar	2 x 15ml spoons castor sugar
Grated nutmeg	Grated nutmeg
3 macaroons	3 macaroons

1. Using a sharp or serrated knife, cut peel from orange, including white pith. Hold orange over a basin, to catch juice; cut out segments. Place one-third of segments in a basin and reserve for slimmer's portion; place remainder in a bowl.

2. Skin bananas and slice. Add to oranges in bowl.

3. Mix sugar with ½ x 2.5ml spoon (¼ level teaspoon) nutmeg. Break macaroons into small pieces. Reserve 3 pieces for slimmer's portion.

4. To serve family portions: Arrange a layer of orange and banana in a glass dish. Sprinkle with nutmeg and sugar mixture and macaroon pieces. Top with a layer of orange and banana. Leave in a cool place for 1 to 2 hours before serving. Serve with Quick 'Cream', Whisked Dessert Topping (see recipes on pages 58 and 56), or double cream. To serve slimmer's portion: Arrange layers of orange segments in a sundae dish. Sprinkle with a pinch of nutmeg and 3 macaroon pieces. Leave in a cool place for 1 to 2 hours before serving.

NOTE: Serves 1 slimmer's portion, 3 family portions.

Valencia Fruit Salad *

For 4 to 6 portions:

IMPERIAL	METRIC
½lb rhubarb	¼kg rhubarb
3 medium-sized oranges	3 medium-sized oranges
Liquid sweetener	Liquid sweetener
4oz grapes	100g grapes
2 pears	2 pears
2 eating apples	2 eating apples

1. Wash and trim rhubarb; cut into 2cm (1in) lengths.

2. Squeeze juice from 2 oranges. Place rhubarb and orange juice in a saucepan; bring to boil, reduce heat, cover and simmer until just tender. Remove from heat; sweeten to taste with liquid sweetener. Leave to cool.

3. Using a sharp or serrated knife, cut peel from remaining orange, including white pith. Slice thinly, then cut slices in halves. Halve grapes; remove pips.

4. Peel, core and slice pears and apples. Place grapes, pears, apples, rhubarb and juice in a serving dish; mix lightly together. Arrange halved orange slices around dish.

Spiced Pears

For 4 portions:

1 large orange
1 medium-sized lemon
Pinch ground ginger
8 sugar substitute tablets or liquid sweetener
4 large dessert pears
4 glacé cherries
Angelica 'leaves'

1. Squeeze juice from orange and lemon; place in a saucepan with 2 x 15ml spoons (2 tablespoons water) ginger and sugar substitute tablets, if used.

2. Peel pears, keeping them whole, and carefully remove core from bases. Place in saucepan, bring to boil, cover and simmer for 20 minutes, turning frequently.

3. Arrange pears on a serving dish. Sweeten liquid in pan to taste with liquid sweetener, if used, then pour liquid over pears. Decorate each pear with a glacé cherry and an angelica 'leaf'. Serve pears hot or cold.

Fruity Lemon Jelly *

For 4 portions:

IMPERIAL	METRIC
2 medium-sized lemons	2 medium-sized lemons
1 level tablespoon gelatine	1 x 15ml spoon gelatine
Liquid sweetener	Liquid sweetener
1 orange	1 orange
1 pear	1 pear
Small bunch of grapes	Small bunch of grapes

1. Scrub lemons. Using a sharp knife or potato peeler, cut peel from 1 lemon, taking care not to include any white pith. Squeeze juice from both lemons and place, with gelatine in a bowl.

2. Place lemon peel and 375ml (¾ pint) water in a saucepan; bring to boil, cover and simmer for 5 minutes. Strain on to lemon juice and gelatine mixture; stir until gelatine has dissolved. Sweeten to taste with liquid sweetener; leave to cool.

3. Using a sharp or serrated knife, cut peel from orange, including white pith. Hold orange over gelatine mixture, to catch juice; cut out segments of orange. Peel, core and chop pear. Cut grapes in halves and remove pips.

4. Place fruit in a 850ml (1½-pint) jelly mould. Add jelly and leave in a cool place until set.

5. Dip mould in hand-hot water, turn out on to a serving dish. Serve with Whisked Dessert Topping or Quick 'Cream' (see recipes on pages 56 and 58).

Snowy Orange Pudding

(pictured on page 45)

For 4 portions:

IMPERIAL	METRIC
1 large orange	1 large orange
1½oz dried skimmed milk	50g dried skimmed milk
Sugar substitute tablets or liquid sweetener	Sugar substitute tablets or liquid sweetener
4 eggs	4 eggs
1 small cooking apple	1 small cooking apple
2 level teaspoons castor sugar (optional)	1 x 10ml spoon castor sugar (optional)

1. Prepare a moderate oven (190 deg C, 375 deg F, Gas Mark 5). Half fill a roasting tin with hot water; place tin in centre of oven.
2. Scrub orange. Using a sharp knife or potato peeler, cut peel from orange, taking care not to include any white pith.
3. Place dried milk in a measuring jug and make up to 400ml (¾ pint) with water. Place milk, orange rind and 8 sugar substitute tables, if used, in a pan; bring to boil; simmer for 5 minutes, stirring.
4. Separate 2 eggs; place whites in a clean, grease-free bowl and yolks in a basin. Add remaining 2 eggs to yolks; beat together. Add milk mixture and 14 drops liquid sweetener, if used, gradually to beaten eggs; beat lightly. Strain egg and milk mixture into a 850ml (1½-pint) ovenproof dish. Place dish in roasting tin; bake for 1¼ hours.
5. Using a sharp or serrated knife, cut pith from orange. Hold orange over a basin, to catch juice, and cut out segments of orange, discarding pips; reserve orange segments and any juice.
6. Peel and slice apple; place sliced apple, 1 x 15ml spoon (1 tablespoon) orange juice and 4 sugar substitute tablets, if used, in a saucepan. Cover and cook gently, stirring occasionally, until apples are soft; beat. Sweeten to taste with liquid sweetener, if used.
7. Whisk egg whites until stiff, but not dry. Whisk in castor sugar, if used, and fold in apple purée. Pile apple meringue on top of custard; arrange reserved orange segments down centre of meringue.

Orange Rice Cloud

For 4 portions:

IMPERIAL	METRIC
1½oz dried skimmed milk	50g dried skimmed molk
1oz ground rice	25g ground rice
1 medium-sized orange	1 medium-sized orange
1 egg	1 egg
Liquid sweetener	Liquid sweetener

1. Place dried skimmed milk in a measuring jug and make up to 400ml (¾ pint) with water. Pour into a saucepan; add ground rice.
2. Scrub orange; grate rind from half of orange and add to milk. Bring to boil, stirring continuously. Reduce heat and cook for 10 minutes, stirring occasionally; remove from heat.
3. Using a sharp or serrated knife, cut peel from orange, including white pith. Hold orange over a basin, to catch juice; cut out segments and reserve for decoration.
4. Separate egg; place white in a clean, grease-free bowl and beat yolk into ground-rice mixture. Cook, stirring continuously, for 1 minute. Remove from heat and sweeten to taste with liquid sweetener. Prepare a hot grill.
5. Whisk egg white until stiff, but not dry. Fold into ground-rice mixture with a metal spoon, until all egg white has been incorporated. Turn out into a warmed ovenproof serving dish and grill until brown. Decorate with orange segments. Serve hot.

Crispy Cinnamon Pears

For 4 portions:

IMPERIAL	METRIC
1½lb cooking pears	¾kg cooking pears
1 medium-sized lemon	1 medium-sized lemon
1 rounded tablespoon golden syrup	2 x 15ml spoons golden syrup

TOPPING	TOPPING
3 slices white bread from a large loaf	3 slices white bread from a large loaf
1oz butter	25g butter
1oz demerara sugar	25g demerara sugar
½ level teaspoon ground cinnamon	1 x 2.5ml spoon ground cinnamon

1. Prepare a moderate oven (190 deg C, 375 deg F, Gas Mark 5).
2. Peel and core pears, slice thinly and place in a 1½-litre (2 to 2½-pint) ovenproof dish.
3. Squeeze juice from lemon and add to dish, with syrup and 2 x 15ml spoons (2 tablespoons) water; cover with foil. Place on a baking sheet in centre of oven and cook until pears are tender, about 30 minutes.
4. To make topping: Remove crusts from bread and cut into tiny dice. Melt butter in a pan; stir in sugar, cinnamon and bread dice.
5. When pears are cooked, place sufficient slices for 1 portion in an individual dish, then sprinkle topping over pears remaining in ovenproof dish. Return dish to oven and cook for a further 15 to 20 minutes, until topping is browned and crisp. Serve hot or cold, with cream or custard for the family portion, and a little top of the milk or Quick 'Cream' (recipe on page 58) for slimmer's portion.

NOTE: Serves 1 slimmer's portion, 3 family portions.

Souffle Apple Omelet

(pictured opposite and on back cover)

For 4 portions:

IMPERIAL	METRIC
2 teaspoons original sharp bottled pure lemon juice	1 x 10ml spoon original sharp bottled pure lemon juice
1 large dessert apple	1 large dessert apple
2 rounded teaspoons clear honey	2 x 10ml spoons clear honey

OMELET	OMELET
4 eggs	4 eggs
Margarine	Margarine
Icing sugar (optional)	Icing sugar (optional)

1. Place lemon juice in a medium-sized saucepan. Peel apple; cut into quarters, core and slice. Place slices in saucepan and coat with lemon juice. Add honey and 1 x 15ml spoon (1 tablespoon) water. Bring to boil; cover, reduce heat and cook gently for 3 to 4 minutes, until apple is just tender.

2. Prepare a moderate grill. Separate eggs; place yolks in a basin and whites in a clean, grease-free bowl. Add 1 x 10ml spoon (2 teaspoons) water to yolks and beat with a fork until smooth.

3. Whisk egg whites until stiff, but not dry; carefully fold in egg yolk mixture, using a metal spoon.

4. Melt a small knob of margarine in a thick-based, 20cm (8in) frying pan over a moderate heat. Pour in egg mixture; spread evenly in pan and cook slowly until sides have just set and underside is golden brown.

5. Place frying pan under grill for 2 to 3 minutes, until omelet is lightly browned and puffs up. Remove from heat and slide on to a warmed serving dish, supporting omelet with a spatula, if necessary.

6. Quickly fill with cooked apple slices and spoon syrup over fruit. Fold over, using spatula. Sprinkle top with a little icing sugar, if desired. Serve immediately, cut into wedges.

ALTERNATIVE FILLINGS FOR OMELET

CHOCOLATE PEAR

IMPERIAL	METRIC
1 large dessert pear	1 large dessert pear
1 level teaspoon cocoa	1 x 5ml spoon cocoa
¼ level teaspoon cinnamon	½ x 2.5ml spoon cinnamon
3 low-calorie sugar cubes	3 low-calorie sugar cubes

1. Peel, core and slice pear.

2. Place cocoa, cinnamon, sugar cubes and 3 tablespoons water in a medium-sized saucepan. Bring to boil, stirring. Reduce heat; add pear slices and gently poach until pears are tender.

3. Fill omelet with pear; spoon syrup over fruit.

HONIED RASPBERRIES

IMPERIAL	METRIC
4oz frozen raspberries	100g frozen raspberries
1 level tablespoon honey	1 x 15ml spoon honey

1. Place raspberries in a basin. Drizzle honey over fruit and leave to thaw.

2. When thawed, gently turn raspberries in juice. Quickly fill omelet with raspberries; spoon juice over fruit.

GINGERED APPLE

IMPERIAL	METRIC
1 tablespoon lemon juice	1 x 15ml spoon lemon juice
1 large dessert apple	1 large dessert apple
2 teaspoons ginger syrup	2 x 5ml spoons ginger syrup

1. Place lemon juice in a small basin.

2. Peel and core apple; cut into small dice. Add to lemon juice and mix well, to coat apple. Stir in ginger syrup and leave for 30 minutes.

3. Fill omelet with apple; spoon over fruit.

SEGMENTED ORANGE

1 large orange

1. Using a sharp or serrated knife, cut peel from orange, including white pith. Hold orange over a basin, to catch juice, then cut out segments and add to juice.

2. Quickly fill omelet with orange segments; spoon juice over fruit.

Australian Baked Apples

For 4 portions:

IMPERIAL	METRIC
4 medium-sized cooking apples	4 medium-sized cooking apples
1oz sultanas	25g sultanas
½ level teaspoon ground cinnamon	1 x 2.5 spoon ground cinnamon
2 level teaspoons honey	4 x 2.5ml spoons honey

1. Prepare a moderate oven (180 deg C, 350 deg F, Gas Mark 4).

2. Wash and core apples. Using a sharp knife, score skin from top to bottom of apples in 4 places. Place apples in a shallow, ovenproof dish or tin, with 4 x 15ml spoons (4 tablespoons) water.

3. In a small basin, mix together sultanas and cinnamon and divide mixture between apples. Top each apple with 1 x 2.5ml spoon (½ teaspoon) honey.

4. Bake, just below centre of oven, for 45 minutes or until tender.

SOUFFLE APPLE OMELET

Quick Apple Crumble *

For 4 portions:

IMPERIAL	METRIC
4 slices starch-reduced bread	4 slices starch-reduced bread
1lb cooking apples	$\frac{1}{2}$kg cooking apples
1 level teaspoon grated lemon rind	1 x 5ml spoon grated lemon rind
Liquid sweetener	Liquid sweetener

1. Prepare a moderate grill. Place starch-reduced bread on grill rack and toast slowly on both sides, until lightly browned and very crisp. Place toast between 2 sheets of greaseproof paper; crush finely, using a rolling pin.
2. Peel, core and thinly slice apples. Place in a saucepan, with 4 x 15ml spoons (4 tablespoons) water. Bring to boil, reduce heat, cover and simmer for 5 to 6 minutes, stirring occasionally, until apple is tender.
3. Remove apple from heat. Stir in lemon rind and 4 or 5 drops of liquid sweetener. Spread apple in bottom of a warmed 20cm ($7\frac{1}{2}$in) ovenproof pie plate. Sprinkle evenly with toasted breadcrumbs.
4. Grill for 3 to 4 minutes, until golden brown. Serve immediately with egg custard or Quick 'Cream' (see recipe on page 58).

Rhubarb Fool

For 4 portions:

IMPERIAL	METRIC
1lb rhubarb	$\frac{1}{2}$kg rhubarb
$\frac{1}{2}$ pint milk	250ml milk
1 rounded tablespoon custard powder	2 x 15ml spoons custard powder
Pink food colouring	Pink food colouring
Liquid sweetener	Liquid sweetener
1 small (5 fluid oz) carton double cream	1 small (142ml) carton double cream

1. Wash and trim rhubarb; cut into short lengths. Place in a saucepan with 3 x 15ml spoons (3 tablespoons) water. Bring to boil, cover and simmer until soft, then rub through a sieve, or make a purée in an electric blender.
2. Blend custard powder and 1 x 15ml spoon (1 tablespoon) milk in a saucepan. Add remainder of milk, bring to boil and cook for 1 to 2 minutes, stirring continuously. Remove from heat, then gradually beat in rhubarb purée.
3. Add a few drops of pink colouring, if necessary. Leave to cool slightly, sweeten to taste with liquid sweetener, then divide between 4 sundae dishes. Leave to cool completely; chill in refrigerator.
4. Whisk cream until stiff; pipe or fork a little cream on top of each fool. Serve with shortbread finger biscuits for the non-slimmers.

Quick 'Bake' Apple

For 4 portions:

IMPERIAL	METRIC
4 medium-sized cooking apples	4 medium-sized cooking apples
2 teaspoons lemon juice	2 x 5ml spoons lemon juice
$\frac{1}{2}$ level teaspoon ground cinnamon	1 x 2.5ml spoon ground cinnamon
1 quantity Quick 'Cream' (see recipe on page 58)	1 quantity Quick 'Cream' (see recipe on page 58)

1. Bring a large saucepan of water to the boil.
2. Wash and core apples. Using a sharp knife, score skin around middle of each apple. Place each apple in centre of a large square of foil. Sprinkle lemon juice and cinnamon into centre of each apple.
3. Mould foil around each apple and twist edges together securely on top, to seal. Place parcels in saucepan of boiling water; cover and simmer for 15 to 20 minutes, until apples are tender.
4. Remove apples from foil and place on a serving dish. Spoon any juices over fruit. Serve hot or cold with Quick 'Cream' (recipe on page 58). If desired, serve castor sugar and single cream for the non-slimmers.

Cherry Delight

For 4 or 5 portions:

IMPERIAL	METRIC
1 level tablespoon custard powder	1 x 15ml spoon custard powder
Dried skimmed milk	Dried skimmed milk
1 small can evaporated milk	1 small can evaporated milk
1 small (8oz) can cherries	1 small (226g) can cherries
Liquid sweetener	Liquid sweetener
1 level tablespoon gelatine	1 x 15ml spoon gelatine
Almond essence	Almond essence
1 sponge flan case	1 sponge flan case
Angelica 'leaves'	Angelica 'leaves'

1. Place custard powder and 25g (1oz) dried skimmed milk in a measuring jug. Make up to 250ml ($\frac{1}{2}$ pint) with water and pour into a small saucepan. Bring to boil, stirring continuously, and cook for 1 to 2 minutes. Remove from heat and cover with a piece of wetted greaseproof paper, to prevent a skin forming; leave to cool.
2. Place evaporated milk in a measuring jug. Add syrup from can of cherries and cold custard; make up to 500ml (1 pint) with reconstituted dried skimmed milk. Pour into a basin and sweeten to taste with liquid sweetener.
3. Measure 3 x 15ml spoons (3 tablespoons) cold water into a small basin; add gelatine and stir. Place basin in a pan of water over a moderate heat; stir until gelatine has dissolved. Add to custard mixture

and mix. Add a few drops of almond essence to taste. Leave until just on the point of setting.

4. Stone cherries. Cut 5 in halves and reserve for decoration; cut remainder into quarters.

5. When custard mixture is beginning to thicken, fold in quartered cherries. When almost set, spoon 1 portion into an individual serving glass. Pour remainder into sponge flan case. Leave until set; decorate with halved cherries and angelica 'leaves'.

NOTE: This serves 1 slimmer's portion and 3 to 4 family portions.

Gooseberry Frou Frou

For 4 portions:

IMPERIAL	METRIC
PASTRY	PASTRY
4oz plain flour	**100g plain flour**
½ level teaspoon salt	**1 x 2.5ml spoon salt**
1oz lard	**25g lard**
1oz margarine	**25g margarine**
Cold water to mix	**Cold water to mix**
FILLING	FILLING
1lb gooseberries	**½kg gooseberries**
2oz to 3oz granulated sugar	**50g to 75g granulated sugar**
1 level tablespoon cornflour	**1 x 15ml spoon cornflour**
2 eggs	**2 eggs**
3oz castor sugar	**75g castor sugar**

1. Prepare a moderately hot oven (200 deg C, 400 deg F, Gas Mark 6). Place a 17.5cm (7in) flan ring on a baking sheet. (Invert baking sheet, if it has a rim.)

2. Place flour and salt in a bowl. Add fats, cut into small pieces and rub in with the fingertips until mixture resembles fine breadcrumbs. Add about 1 x 15ml spoon (1 tablespoon) cold water and mix with a fork to form a firm dough.

3. Roll out pastry to a circle, 4cm (1½in) larger all round than flan ring. Roll pastry around rolling pin and lift on to flan ring. Gently ease pastry into flan ring and press into base of ring with the fingers. Roll off surplus pastry with a rolling pin across top of flan. Prick all over base with a fork. Place a circle of greaseproof paper in flan; fill with baking beans or rice. Place in centre of oven and bake for 15 minutes. Remove paper and beans or rice. Return flan to oven and cook for a further 5 minutes; remove flan ring.

4. Reduce oven temperature to cool (170 deg C, 325 deg F, Gas Mark 3).

5. Top and tail gooseberries; place in a saucepan with 1 tablespoon water and granulated sugar; cover and cook until tender. Remove from heat.

6. Blend cornflour with a little cold water and stir into gooseberries. Return to heat, bring to boil, stirring, and cook for 3 to 4 minutes.

7. Separate eggs; place whites in a clean, grease-free basin and add yolks to gooseberries and mix together well.

8. Place a small ovenproof dish on baking sheet with flan case (for slimmer's portion).

9. Place three-quarters of gooseberry mixture in flan case and the remainder into small dish.

10. Whisk egg whites until stiff, add half the castor sugar and continue whisking until stiff again. Fold in remaining sugar, using a metal spoon.

11. Place meringue in a nylon piping bag fitted with a large star tube and pipe stars of meringue over both dishes, or pile on both; swirl with a fork.

12. Place in centre of oven and cook for 30 minutes until meringue is tinged golden brown.

13. Place flan on a serving dish and the individual dish on a plate. Serve warm or cold.

NOTE: Serves 1 slimmer's portion, 3 family portions.

Vanilla Ice *

For 4 portions:

IMPERIAL	METRIC
1 level teaspoon gelatine	**1 x 5ml spoon gelatine**
6 level tablespoons dried skimmed milk	**6 x 15ml spoons dried skimmed milk**
½ teaspoon vanilla essence	**1 x 2.5ml spoon vanilla essence**
Liquid sweetener	**Liquid sweetener**

1. Turn refrigerator to coldest setting. Measure 1 tablespoon cold water into a small basin; add gelatine and stir. Place basin in a pan of water over a moderate heat; stir until gelatine has dissolved.

2. Place dried skimmed milk in a measuring jug and make up to 175ml (6 fluid ounces) with water. Stir in vanilla essence and dissolved gelatine. Pour into a basin; chill and leave until on the point of setting.

3. Remove milk mixture from refrigerator. Using an electric whisk or rotary beater, whisk until thick, very white, fluffy and almost doubled in volume. Sweeten to taste with liquid sweetener. Pour into a freezing or plastic tray and place in frozen food compartment of refrigerator; freeze for 1 hour or until firm. Turn refrigerator back to normal setting.

NOTE: For Ginger Ice (pictured on page 68): Omit vanilla essence and add 1 piece finely-chopped stem ginger and 1 teaspoon stem-ginger syrup. For Coffee Ice: Omit vanilla essence and add 1 rounded teaspoon instant coffee to dissolved gelatine. For Chocolate Ice: Omit vanilla essence and dissolve 3 level teaspoons cocoa in 2 tablespoons boiling water. Add dried skimmed milk, beat well and make up to 175ml (6 fluid oz) with water. For Raspberry Ice: Omit vanilla essence. Fold 50g (2oz) crushed fresh or frozen raspberries and a few drops of red food colouring, if desired, into whisked mixture before freezing.

RHUBARB WITH GINGER
ICE (a variation
of Vanilla Ice, see
recipe on page 67)

ORANGE CHEESECAKE

Mocha Orange Dessert

For 4 portions:

IMPERIAL	METRIC
¾ pint milk	375ml milk
2 level tablespoons dried skimmed milk	2 x 15ml spoons dried skimmed milk
2 level tablespoons cocoa	2 x 15ml spoons cocoa
1 level tablespoon instant coffee	1 x 15ml spoon instant coffee
12 sugar substitute tablets or liquid sweetener	12 sugar substitute tablets or liquid sweetener
3 eggs	3 eggs
1 level tablespoon gelatine	1 x 15ml spoon gelatine
1 (5.3oz) carton natural low-fat yoghourt	1 (150ml) carton natural low-fat yoghourt
1 (11oz) can mandarin oranges	1 (312g) can mandarin oranges

1. Place milk, dried milk, cocoa, coffee and sugar substitute tablets, if used, in a saucepan. Heat gently until almost boiling; remove from heat. Separate eggs; place whites in a clean, grease-free bowl and beat egg yolks in a basin. Pour milk mixture on to egg yolks, stirring; return to the saucepan and stir over a very low heat, until custard thickens (do not allow to boil).

2. Measure 3 x 15ml spoons (3 tablespoons) cold water into a small basin; add gelatine and stir. Place basin in a pan of water over a moderate heat and stir until gelatine has dissolved. Add gelatine to custard and stir well. Sweeten to taste with liquid sweetener, if used. Cool, then leave in refrigerator until mixture is just on the point of setting.

3. Whisk egg whites until stiff, but not dry. Fold egg whites into custard, using a metal spoon. Pour into 4 individual glasses and leave to set.

4. Just before serving, pour yoghourt over each dessert and decorate with well-drained mandarin oranges.

Orange Cheesecake

(pictured on pages 68, 69)

For 6 portions:

IMPERIAL	METRIC
5 starch-reduced digestive biscuits	5 starch-reduced digestive biscuits
1 large orange	1 large orange
Half a medium-sized lemon	Half a medium-sized lemon
1 level tablespoon gelatine	1 x 15ml spoon gelatine
1 large (8oz) carton cottage cheese	1 large (226g) carton cottage cheese
3 level tablespoons dried skimmed milk	3 x 15ml spoons dried skimmed milk
12 drops liquid sweetener	12 drops liquid sweetener

1. Place biscuits between 2 sheets of greaseproof paper; crush finely with a rolling pin. Lightly butter a round 15cm (6in) loose-based cake tin. Place 2 x 15ml spoons (2 tablespoons) biscuit crumbs in tin and toss until coated. Hold bottom of tin and invert, to remove excess crumbs; reserve.

2. Scrub orange and lemon. Grate 1 x 5ml spoon (1 level teaspoon) rind from half the orange and rind from half lemon; reserve. Cut orange in half; reserve half with rind for decoration. Squeeze juice from remaining half orange and place in a measuring jug. Make up to 125ml (¼ pint) with water. Squeeze juice from lemon and add to jug. Add gelatine and stir. Place jug in a pan of water over a moderate heat and stir until gelatine has dissolved.

3. Place cottage cheese in a sieve over a bowl. Rub cheese through sieve with a wooden spoon. Add dissolved gelatine, dried skimmed milk, liquid sweetener and 2 x 15ml spoons (2 tablespoons) water to bowl. Beat together until smooth. Leave in refrigerator until on the point of setting.

4. Using an electric whisk or rotary beater, whisk the cheese mixture for 1 to 2 minutes, until light and smooth. Lightly whisk in reserved orange and lemon rind. Pour into tin and sprinkle top with reserved biscuit crumbs, to coat. Leave in refrigerator until set.

5. To remove cheesecake from tin: Place tin on top of a 425g-size (1lb) can; gently pull cake tin down from cheesecake. Ease cheesecake off base on to a plate with a palette knife.

6. To decorate: Cut 4 slices from reserved orange half. Cut 3 slices in quarters; arrange around top edge of cheesecake. Cut remaining slice through to centre, twist and place in centre of cheesecake.

NOTE: Alternatively, place cottage cheese, dissolved gelatine, liquid sweetener, dried skimmed milk and 2 x 15ml spoons (2 tablespoons) water in a liquidiser goblet. Run machine until well blended. Pour into a bowl and continue as from step 4.

ENTERTAINING

MENU FOR

INFORMAL DINNER

Cucumber Cocktail Soup
(recipe on page 27)
Egg and Fish Florentine
Parsleyed Turnips
Green Beans
Pear and Orange Cloud

Egg and Fish Florentine

For 4 portions:

IMPERIAL	METRIC
2 eggs	2 eggs
2 small (8oz) cartons frozen spinach	2 small (227g) cartons frozen spinach
1 large packet (4) frozen cod steaks	1 large packet (4) frozen cod steaks
2 medium-sized tomatoes	2 medium-sized tomatoes
4oz Edam cheese	100g Edam cheese
Milk	Milk
Salt and pepper	Salt and pepper
$\frac{1}{4}$ level teaspoon made mustard	$\frac{1}{2}$ x 2.5ml spoon made mustard
2 level teaspoons cornflour	1 x 10ml spoon cornflour
Paprika (optional)	Paprika (optional)

---

1. Hard boil eggs for 10 minutes; crack and leave to cool in cold water. Shell and dry on kitchen paper. Cook spinach, as directed on carton. Prepare a moderate grill.

2. Place cod steaks on grill rack and grill for 10 minutes. Cut tomatoes in halves; place on grill rack. Turn cod steaks; grill tomatoes and cod steaks for a further 5 minutes. Grate cheese; place in a small saucepan, with 2 x 15ml spoons (2 tablespoons) milk, a pinch of salt, a shake of pepper and the mustard. Stir over a low heat until melted.

3. Blend cornflour and 2 x 15ml spoons (2 tablespoons) milk together. Stir into cheese. Bring to boil, stirring, then remove from heat.

4. Drain spinach, if necessary. Place on a warmed serving dish. Arrange cod steaks on spinach. Cut eggs in halves lengthwise; place a half on each cod steak, rounded side uppermost. Spoon cheese sauce over. Arrange tomato halves between cod steaks.

5. Sprinkle sauce with a little paprika, if desired. Serve with Parsleyed Turnips and green beans.

Parsleyed Turnips *

For 4 portions:

IMPERIAL	METRIC
1lb turnips	$\frac{1}{2}$kg turnips
Chopped parsley	Chopped parsley

Peel turnips; cut into 1cm ($\frac{1}{2}$in) cubes. Cook in boiling, salted water until just tender, about 15 minutes; drain. Place in a warmed serving dish and sprinkle with chopped parsley.

Pear and Orange Cloud *

For 4 portions:

IMPERIAL	METRIC
2 large dessert pears	2 large dessert pears
$\frac{1}{4}$ pint undiluted low-calorie orange drink	125ml undiluted low-calorie orange drink
1 level tablespoon gelatine	1 x 15ml spoon gelatine
4 rounded tablespoons dried skimmed milk	125ml dried skimmed milk
Liquid sweetener	Liquid sweetener

---

1. Peel, quarter and core pears. Cut into 1cm ($\frac{1}{2}$in) cubes and place in a small saucepan. Add half the orange drink and 4 x 15ml spoons (4 tablespoons) water. Cover and cook over a low heat, until pears are tender.

2. Drain pears, reserving pear juice. Reserve 2 x 15ml spoons (1 rounded tablespoon) cubed pear for decoration; place remainder in 4 glasses.

3. Make up pear juice to 250ml ($\frac{1}{2}$ pint) with remaining orange drink and water. Measure 3 x 15ml (3 tablespoons) of the juice into a small basin; add gelatine and stir. Place basin in a pan of water over a moderate heat and stir until gelatine has dissolved. Remove from heat; stir in remaining juice. Leave in a cool place until on the point of setting.

4. Place dried milk in a measuring jug; make up to 125ml ($\frac{1}{4}$ pint) with cold water. Stir in about 16 drops liquid sweetener (or the equivalent of 25g (1oz) sugar). When jelly has just set, whisk with a rotary whisk until light; gradually whisk in milk mixture. Leave for a few minutes, to set; divide between glasses. Place a little reserved pear on each glass.

EGG AND FISH FLORENTINE
PARSLEYED TURNIPS
PEAR AND ORANGE CLOUD

MENU FOR

Chicken Liver Pâté

Country Potted Tuna

Picuto Salad

Bowl of Fresh Vegetables

Piquant Dip

Tomato Dip

Country Cottage Dip

Green Salad

*   *

Raspberry Petal Dessert

(*recipe on page* 56)

Orange Dream Cups

(*recipe on page* 56)

Lime Tea Punch

(*recipe on page* 87)

Piquant Dip *

IMPERIAL	METRIC
3 rounded tablespoons low-calorie vinegar and oil dressing	6 x 15ml spoons low-calorie vinegar and oil dressing
4 black olives	4 black olives
2 level tablespoons capers	2 x 15ml spoons capers
4 gherkins	4 gherkins

1. Place vinegar and oil dressing in a basin.
2. Remove stones from olives; chop olives, capers and gherkins finely. Add to dressing and mix well; pour into a glass serving dish.

Chicken Liver Pâté *

(pictured on page 76)

For 8 portions:

IMPERIAL	METRIC
¾lb chicken livers	350g chicken livers
1 small onion	1 small onion
1 small clove of garlic	1 small clove of garlic
Margarine	Margarine
½ level teaspoon salt	1 x 2.5ml spoon salt
1 small (8oz) can tomatoes	1 small (226g) can tomatoes
1 teaspoon Worcestershire sauce	1 x 5ml spoon Worcestershire sauce
½ level teaspoon meat extract	1 x 2.5 ml spoon meat extract
Pepper	Pepper
4oz cooked chicken	100g cooked chicken
Parsley	Parsley
¼ level teaspoon caraway seeds (optional)	½ x 2.5ml spoon caraway seeds (optional)
1 egg	1 egg

GARNISH	GARNISH
Shredded lettuce	Shredded lettuce
Cucumber	Cucumber

1. Prepare a cool oven (170 deg C, 325 deg F, Gas Mark 3). Half fill a roasting tin with cold water.
2. Cut chicken livers into small pieces. Peel and chop onion and garlic. Melt a small knob of margarine in a saucepan. Add garlic, onion, chicken livers and salt; fry gently for 2 minutes. Discard 3 x 15 ml spoons (3 tablespoons) juice from can of tomatoes; add tomatoes and remaining juice to pan with Worcestershire sauce, meat extract and a shake of pepper. Bring to boil, cover and simmer for 10 minutes, stirring occasionally; leave to cool slightly.
3. Place contents of pan in a liquidiser goblet. Add chicken, a sprig of parsley, caraway seeds, if used, and egg. Run machine until contents are well blended. (Alternatively, remove liver, onion and garlic from pan, using a draining spoon. Reserve liquor in pan and finely mince liver, onion, garlic, chicken and parsley. Add to liquor in pan. Beat egg; add to pan with caraway seeds, if used; mix well.)
4. Place liver mixture in a ½ kg (1 lb), ¾ litre, 1½-pint capacity) loaf tin; cover with foil. Cook in centre of oven for 2 hours. Take loaf tin out of water; remove foil and leave pâté to become cold.
5. Turn pâté carefully out of tin and place on a serving dish. Garnish dish with shredded lettuce. Cut 6 thin of cucumber; cut each slice through to centre. Fold around to make a cone; press firmly. Arrange cones on top of pâté.

6. Serve pâté, cut into slices, with toasted starch reduced bread or crispbread, and low-fat spread.

NOTE: This pâté is best if made 1 to 2 days in advance. Remove from tin, wrap in foil or self-clinging plastic wrap and store in refrigerator.

Country Potted Tuna

(pictured on page 76)

For 8 portions:

IMPERIAL	METRIC
½lb cod fillet	¼kg cod fillet
1 small onion	1 small onion
Half a medium-sized lemon	Half a medium-sized lemon
½ level teaspoon salt	1 x 2.5ml spoon salt
Pepper	Pepper
2 level teaspoons cornflour	1 x 10ml spoon cornflour
¼ level teaspoon dry mustard	½ x 2.5ml spoon dry mustard
¼ level teaspoon Cayenne pepper	½ x 2.5ml spoon Cayenne pepper
1 large (7½oz) can tuna	1 large (213g) can tuna

GLAZE	GLAZE
1 level teaspoon gelatine	1 x 5ml spoon gelatine
½ teaspoon Worcestershire sauce	1 x 2.5ml spoon Worcestershire sauce

Sprig of parsley	Sprig of parsley

1. Remove skin from fish. Peel and finely chop onion. Cut 2 slices from lemon and reserve; squeeze juice from remaining pieces of lemon and place in a medium-sized saucepan with fish, onion, salt, a shake of pepper and 125ml (¼ pint) water.

2. Bring to boil; reduce heat, cover and simmer for 6 to 7 minutes, until fish is cooked. Remove fish from pan, using a draining spoon, and drain thoroughly; reserve liquor in pan. Place fish in a bowl; flake with a fork. Remove any bones and leave fish to cool.

3. Blend cornflour, mustard and Cayenne pepper with a little of reserved liquor. Stir into liquor in pan. Bring to boil, stirring continuously, and cook for 1 minute, until thickened; leave to cool.

4. Drain oil from can of tuna. Add cooled sauce and tuna to flaked fish. Mix well with a fork and press mixture lightly into a ½ litre (1 pint) shallow serving dish. Level top and chill in refrigerator.

5. Measure 3 x 15ml spoons (3 tablespoons) cold water into a small basin; add gelatine and stir. Place basin in a pan of water over a moderate heat;

stir until gelatine has dissolved. Remove basin from heat; stir in Worcester sauce. Leave until cool, but not set.

6. Cut reserved lemon slices in quarters and arrange on top of fish mixture. Pour gelatine over surface; chill until set. Garnish with a sprig of parsley.

Picuto Salad *

(pictured on page 76)

For 8 portions:

6 large tomatoes
12 pickled baby dill cucumbers
Lemon juice
Salt
Black pepper
Chopped parsley

1. Slice tomatoes and pickled dill cucumbers. Arrange slices of tomato, overlapping, around edge of a serving plate. Pile sliced cucumber in centre.

2. Sprinkle tomato and cucumber with a little lemon juice, salt, black pepper and chopped parsley.

Bowl of Fresh Vegetables *

Arrange sticks of carrot, cucumber and celery in a bowl with quartered tomatoes, radishes and sliced, white cabbage. Serve with dips.

Country Cottage Dip *

IMPERIAL	METRIC
4oz cottage cheese with chives	100g cottage cheese with chives
1 (5.3oz) carton natural low-fat yoghourt	1 (150g) carton natural low-fat yoghourt
1 medium-sized carrot	1 medium-sized carrot

1. Mix cottage cheese and yoghourt in a basin.

2. Peel carrot and grate finely into cheese mixture; mix together and pour into a glass serving dish.

Tomato Dip *

IMPERIAL	METRIC
3 rounded tablespoons low-calorie vinegar and oil dressing	6 x 15ml spoons low-calorie vinegar and oil dressing
3 level tablespoons tomato purée	3 x 15ml spoons tomato purée

Blend vinegar and oil dressing and tomato purée together in a basin. Pour into a glass serving dish.

BUFFET PARTY: CHICKEN
LIVER PATE and
PICUTO SALAD (in fore-
ground), with COUNTRY
POTTED TUNA and LIME TEA
PUNCH (at back)

ORIENTAL SUPPER: Reading clockwise are:
PEARL BALLS IN SWEET AND SOUR SAUCE,
CLEAR EGG SOUP, BOILED CHICKEN WITH
MUSHROOMS and BEAN SPROUT RICE.
Serve Stewed Rhubarb with Ginger Ice
(pictured on page 68 as a dessert)

MENU FOR

ORIENTAL SUPPER

Clear Egg Soup
Boiled Chicken with Mushrooms
Pearl Balls in Sweet and Sour Sauce
Bean Sprout Rice
Fresh Fruit

or

Stewed Rhubarb with Ginger Ice
(*see recipe for Vanilla Ice on page* 67)

Clear Egg Soup *

(pictured on page 77)

For 4 to 6 portions:

IMPERIAL	METRIC
2 pints chicken stock (reserved from Boiled Chicken with Mushrooms)	1 litre chicken stock (reserved from Boiled Chicken with Mushrooms)
1 stick of celery	1 stick of celery
1 chicken stock cube	1 chicken stock cube
Half a bunch of watercress	Half a bunch of watercress
2 teaspoons milk	1 x 10ml spoon milk
Beaten egg (reserved from Pearl Balls)	Beaten egg (reserved from Pearl Balls)
Salt and pepper	Salt and pepper

1. Bring reserved stock to boil. Wash and thinly slice celery; add to saucepan, with stock cube. Cover and simmer for 5 minutes.

2. Wash watercress thoroughly; add to saucepan after 4 minutes. Add milk to reserved beaten egg. Remove saucepan from heat and slowly pour egg mixture into soup, to form strands of cooked egg.

Taste and season with salt and pepper, if necessary. Pour soup into warmed serving bowls and serve.

NOTE: Stock may be replaced by 1 litre (2 pints) water and 1 extra chicken stock cube. Add 1 small, finely-sliced onion, shake of garlic salt and a little soy sauce to taste.

Bean Sprout Rice *

(pictured on page 77)

For 4 portions:

IMPERIAL	METRIC
4oz long-grain rice	100g long-grain rice
1 ($9\frac{1}{4}$oz) can bean sprouts	1 (246g) can bean sprouts

1. Cook rice in a medium-sized saucepan of boiling, salted water for about 12 minutes. Test by pressing a grain between thumb and finger.

2. Meanwhile, drain liquor from can of bean sprouts; rinse bean sprouts in cold water. Add to rice; return to boil. Drain in a sieve or colander; rinse with hot water. Turn out rice into a warmed serving dish and serve.

Boiled Chicken with Mushrooms *

(pictured on page 77)

For 4 portions:

IMPERIAL	METRIC
1 small onion	1 small onion
1 clove of garlic	1 clove of garlic
Salt	Salt
2 large chicken portions	2 large chicken portions
Soy sauce	Soy sauce
4 medium-sized carrots	4 medium-sized carrots
4oz button mushrooms	100g button mushrooms
1in piece of cucumber	3cm piece of cucumber
$\frac{1}{2}$ teaspoon sesame seeds (optional)	1 x 2.5ml spoon sesame seeds (optional)
$\frac{1}{2}$ teaspoon tabasco sauce	1 x 2.5ml spoon tabasco sauce
1 level teaspoon cornflour	1 x 5ml spoon cornflour
Pepper	Pepper

1. Peel and finely chop onion. Peel clove of garlic; place on a saucer with 1 x 5ml spoon (1 level teaspoon) salt. Using a round-ended knife, rub salt against garlic to crush clove.

2. Remove skin from chicken; place chicken in a large saucepan with garlic, onion, 1 x 10ml spoon (2 teaspoons) soy sauce and $1\frac{1}{4}$ litres ($2\frac{1}{4}$ pints) cold water. Bring to boil, reduce heat, cover and simmer for 15 to 20 minutes. Remove chicken from pan; reserve stock. Leave chicken to cool. Remove meat from bone in even-sized pieces. Add any small pieces of chicken to stock.

3. Peel carrots and cut into small pieces. Wash and halve mushrooms. Cut cucumber into 4 slices; cut slices in halves.

4. To make sauce: Measure 125ml ($\frac{1}{4}$ pint) reserved stock into a small saucepan (reserve remaining stock for Soup). Add carrot, 1 x 2.5ml spoon ($\frac{1}{2}$ teaspoon) soy sauce, sesame seeds, if used, and tabasco sauce. Bring to boil, cover and simmer for 10 minutes.

5. Blend cornflour with 1 x 15ml spoon (1 tablespoon) cold water; add to pan with mushrooms. Bring to boil and cook for 1 minute, stirring continuously. Add chicken; reheat gently in sauce for 2 to 3 minutes. Taste and season with salt and pepper. Arrange chicken and sauce on a warmed serving dish and garnish with cucumber pieces. Serve with a small dish of tabasco sauce.

Pearl Balls in Sweet and Sour Sauce *

(pictured on page 77)

For 4 portions:

IMPERIAL	METRIC
PEARL BALLS	PEARL BALLS
1oz long-grain rice	25g long-grain rice
6oz cod or coley fillet	150g cod or coley fillet
1 teaspoon soy sauce	1 x 5ml spoon soy sauce
Plain flour	Plain flour
Garlic salt	Garlic salt
Salt and pepper	Salt and pepper
1 egg	1 egg
SAUCE	SAUCE
Half a large green pepper	Half a large green pepper
$\frac{1}{4}$ pint natural pineapple juice	150ml natural pineapple juice
1 tablespoon lemon juice	1 x 15ml spoon lemon juice
$\frac{1}{2}$ teaspoon soy sauce	1 x 2.5ml spoon soy sauce
4oz frozen prawns, just thawed	100g frozen prawns, just thawed
1 level teaspoon cornflour	1 x 5ml spoon cornflour

1. Cook rice in a small saucepan of boiling, salted water for 5 minutes; drain well. Spread evenly on kitchen paper; leave to cool.

2. Remove skin from fish; cut fish into small pieces and remove any bones. Place fish, 1 x 5ml spoon (1 teaspoon) soy sauce, 1 x 15ml spoon (1 level tablespoon) flour, a pinch of garlic salt and a little salt and pepper in a basin. Mix well with a fork. Beat egg. Add sufficient beaten egg to fish mixture to bind together. (Reserve remaining egg for Clear Egg Soup.)

3. Lightly flour the hands. Divide fish equally and roll lightly between palms of hands, to make 12 fish balls. Coat each ball with rice.

4. Prepare a steamer. Place a piece of kitchen paper in top compartment; place fish balls, well apart, in steamer. Cover and steam for 15 to 20 minutes, until rice is tender.

5. To make sauce: Cut green pepper into small pieces. Place in a small saucepan, with pineapple juice, lemon juice, 1 x 2.5ml spoon ($\frac{1}{2}$ teaspoon) soy sauce and prawns. Bring to boil, reduce heat and cook for 1 minute. Blend cornflour in a basin with 1 x 5ml spoon (1 teaspoon) water. Stir into sauce and cook for 1 minute, until slightly thickened.

6. Place pearl balls on a warmed serving dish. Cover with sauce and keep hot until ready to serve.

MENU FOR
GARDEN LUNCH

Savoury Swiss Roll
Green Salad with Slimmers' Salad Dressing
Strawberry and Orange Cups
Fresh Lemonade
(*recipe on page* 87)

Savoury Swiss Roll

(pictured opposite and on back cover)

For 4 portions:

IMPERIAL	METRIC
SWISS ROLL	SWISS ROLL
1 small (6oz) carton frozen chopped spinach, just thawed	1 small (170g) carton frozen chopped spinach, just thawed
1 level teaspoon salt	1 x 5ml spoon salt
Pepper	Pepper
1 level teaspoon grated Parmesan cheese	1 x 5ml spoon grated Parmesan cheese
4 eggs	4 eggs
SAUCE	SAUCE
1 rounded tablespoon dried skimmed milk	2 x 15ml spoons dried skimmed milk
2oz button mushrooms	50g button mushrooms
1oz margarine	25g margarine
1oz plain flour	25g plain flour
6oz cottage cheese	150g cottage cheese
½ level teaspoon salt	1 x 2.5ml spoon salt
Pepper	Pepper
Tomato wedges	Tomato wedges

1. Prepare a moderate oven (190 deg C, 375 deg F, Gas Mark 5). Brush an 29cm by 19cm (11in by 7in) Swiss-roll tin with melted fat or oil. Draw around base of tin on greaseproof paper. Cut paper 2cm (½in) out from line; crease paper on line. Press paper down into tin; grease paper.

2. Place thawed spinach in a sieve; using the back of a wooden spoon, press to remove excess liquid. Place spinach in a basin and add salt, a shake of pepper and Parmesan cheese; mix together well.

3. Separate eggs; place whites in a clean, grease-free bowl and beat yolks into spinach mixture.

4. Whisk egg whites until stiff, but not dry; fold into spinach mixture, cutting through with a metal spoon, until all egg white has been incorporated.

5. Pour into prepared tin and bake just above centre of oven for 10 to 15 minutes. Test by pressing with the fingers. If cooked, mixture should feel firm.

6. To make sauce: Place dried skimmed milk in a measuring jug and make up to 125ml (¼ pint) with water. Wash and slice mushrooms. Melt margarine in a medium-sized saucepan, stir in flour and cook gently for 2 minutes, without browning. Add milk; bring to boil, stirring continuously, and simmer for 2 minutes. Stir in cottage cheese, salt and a shake of pepper; cook for a further 2 minutes.

7. Invert spinach mixture on to a sheet of grease-proof paper; remove paper carefully. Spread sauce over spinach mixture. Reserve 5 mushroom slices for garnish and arrange remaining slices over sauce. Roll up firmly from top with the aid of the paper.

8. Place on a warmed serving dish and garnish with tomato wedges and reserved mushroom slices. Serve hot or cold with onion and cucumber salad, or Green Salad with Slimmers' Salad Dressing.

please turn to page 82

SAVOURY SWISS ROLL
STRAWBERRY
AND ORANGE CUPS

Green Salad with Slimmers' Salad Dressing *

For 4 or 5 portions:

IMPERIAL	METRIC
1 lettuce	1 lettuce
1 bunch of watercress	1 bunch of watercress
Half a cucumber	Half a cucumber
1 bunch of spring onions	1 bunch of spring onions

IMPERIAL	METRIC
3 level tablespoons natural low-fat yoghourt	3 x 15ml spoons natural low-fat yoghourt
2 tablespoons bottled pure lemon juice	2 x 15ml spoons bottled pure lemon juice
Salt and pepper	Salt and pepper

1. Remove and discard outer leaves from lettuce. Wash well, shake off excess water; drain well. Pull lettuce leaves from stem; place in a glass or wooden salad bowl.
2. Remove and discard any discoloured leaves from watercress and trim off stalks; wash leaves and drain well. Divide into sprigs and add to lettuce.
3. Wipe and thinly slice cucumber (remove skin, if desired) and add to lettuce.
4. Remove outer skin and roots from onions; wash and dry on kitchen paper. Place onions in a bowl; mix well.
5. To make dressing: Mix together yoghourt, lemon juice and some salt and pepper in a small basin. Serve separately, with salad.

Strawberry and Orange Cups *

(pictured on page 81)

For 4 portions:

IMPERIAL	METRIC
¼lb strawberries	100g strawberries
2 large oranges	2 large oranges
Liquid sweetener (optional)	Liquid sweetener (optional)

1. Wash strawberries and reserve 4 for decoration. Hull remainder; cut into quarters; place in a bowl.
2. Scrub oranges; cut each in half horizontally. Using a sharp or serrated knife, cut around each orange half between flesh and pith. Holding orange over strawberries in bowl, cut between segments. Carefully lift out segments with a spoon and lightly mix with strawberries. Add a few drops of liquid sweetener, to taste, if used.
3. Remove pith and reserve orange shells.
4. Divide fruit equally between orange shells and top each with a reserved strawberry. Chill before serving, if desired.

Shrimp Cocktail *

For a summer dinner party, serve Shrimp Cocktail at the start of this menu.

For 4 to 6 portions:

IMPERIAL	METRIC
A few lettuce leaves	A few lettuce leaves
1 large tomato	1 large tomato
1in piece of cucumber	2cm piece of cucumber
1 (7¼oz) can shrimps	1 (205g) can shrimps

DRESSING	DRESSING
4 level tablespoons low-calorie vinegar and oil dressing	4 x 15ml spoons low-calorie vinegar and oil dressing
2 teaspoons Worcestershire sauce	1 x 10ml spoon Worcestershire sauce
¼ level teaspoon salt	½ x 2.5ml spoon salt
Pepper	Pepper

GARNISH	GARNISH
1 medium-sized lemon	1 medium-sized lemon
Sprigs of watercress	Sprigs of watercress

1. Shred lettuce leaves finely and place in bottom of 4 or 6 small glasses.
2. Place tomato in a basin; cover with boiling water and leave for 1 minute. Drain, then peel and chop. Cut cucumber into small dice; drain can of shrimps.
3. To make dressing: Place low-calorie vinegar and oil dressing in a basin. Add Worcestershire sauce, salt, and a shake of pepper; beat well.
4. Place 2 x 15ml spoons (1 rounded tablespoon) of dressing in a basin; add shrimps, chopped tomato and half the diced cucumber. Mix well and divide between glasses. Spoon remaining sauce over shrimp mixture. Top with remaining cucumber.
5. Cut a slice from each end of lemon; cut lemon in half, lengthwise. Wrap one half in self-clinging plastic wrap and store in a refrigerator for future use. Cut remaining half into 4 or 6 segments, lengthwise. Using a sharp knife, make a cut almost through, between peel and flesh, from one end of each segment. Place one segment on rim of each glass, peel side facing outwards. Garnish each glass with a small sprig of watercress. Serve with fingers of toasted starch-reduced bread, crispbreads and low-fat spread, if desired.

DRINKS

Reading clockwise are:
LEMON TEA, FROTHY
HOT MOCHA, HOT COFFEE
NOG, WHIPPED EGG
WARMER, HOT TOMATO COCK-
TAIL, CREAMY PEA
SOUP and CITRUS CUP

Lemon Tea *

Makes 3 glasses:

IMPERIAL	METRIC
1 tea bag	1 tea bag
Boiling water	Boiling water
3 slices lemon or 3 teaspoons bottled pure lemon juice	3 slices lemon or 3 x 5ml spoons bottled pure lemon juice
Liquid sweetener	Liquid sweetener

1. Make tea, using tea bag and about 250ml (½ pint) boiling water; infuse tea bag for 5 minutes.
2. Divide tea equally between 3 heatproof glasses. Dilute to taste with boiling water; add a slice of lemon or 1 teaspoon lemon juice to each glass. Sweeten to taste, if desired, with liquid sweetener.

Frothy Hot Mocha

For 1 portion:

IMPERIAL	METRIC
2 rounded tablespoons dried skimmed milk	4 x 15ml spoons dried skimmed milk
1 level teaspoon instant coffee	1 x 5ml spoons instant coffee
1 level teaspoon cocoa	1 x 5ml spoon cocoa
Liquid sweetener	Liquid sweetener

Place dried milk, coffee and cocoa in a saucepan; add 250ml (½ pint) water and bring to boil, stirring. Reduce heat and whisk until light and frothy, using a rotary whisk. Sweeten to taste with sweetener. Pour into a 250ml (½ pint) mug; serve immediately.

Hot Coffee Nog *

Makes 2 glasses:

IMPERIAL	METRIC
1 egg	1 egg
Liquid sweetener	Liquid sweetener
1 rounded teaspoon instant coffee	2 x 5ml spoons instant coffee
2 rounded tablespoons dried skimmed milk	4 x 15ml spoons dried skimmed milk
Ground cinnamon or nutmeg (optional)	Ground cinnamon or nutmeg (optional)

1. Separate egg; place white in a clean, grease-free basin, and yolk in a saucepan. Add 2 drops of sweetener to yolk and beat with a wooden spoon.
2. Place coffee and dried milk in a measuring jug; make up to 250ml (½ pint) with water. Add to saucepan. Heat, stirring continuously, until liquid thickens slightly (do not boil); remove from heat.
3. Add 2 drops of sweetener to egg white and whisk until it just forms soft peaks. Divide equally between 2 250ml (½ pint) heatproof glasses. Pour coffee mixture into each glass. Sprinkle each with a little cinnamon or nutmeg, if desired. Serve hot.

Whipped Egg Warmer *

(pictured on page 85)

Makes 3 glasses:

IMPERIAL	METRIC
2oz dried skimmed milk	50g dried skimmed milk
Vanilla essence	Vanilla essence
Liquid sweetener	Liquid sweetener
1 egg	1 egg
Ground nutmeg	Ground nutmeg

1. Place dried milk in a measuring jug; make up to ½ litre (1 pint) with water. Pour into a saucepan and heat until almost boiling; add a few drops of vanilla essence and sweetener to taste.
2. Place egg in measuring jug and whisk until stiff. Divide equally between 3 small heatproof glasses.
3. Pour hot milk into each glass; sprinkle each with nutmeg; serve hot.
NOTE: Alternatively, if not on reducing diet, omit vanilla essence and stir 1 x 15ml spoon (1 level tablespoon) cocoa into milk before heating.

Honied Lemon Nightcap

For 1 portion:

IMPERIAL	METRIC
2 dessertspoons bottled pure lemon juice	2 x 10ml spoons bottled pure lemon juice
1 level teaspoon clear honey	1 x 5ml spoon clear honey
Liquid sweetener (optional)	Liquid sweetener (optional)

Place lemon juice and honey in 250ml (½-pint) beaker or mug. Fill up mug with boiling water. Sweeten with liquid sweetener, if desired.

Vanilla Milk Punch *

For 1 portion:

IMPERIAL	METRIC
2 rounded tablespoons dried skimmed milk	4 x 15ml spoons dried skimmed milk
Boiling water	Boiling water
Vanilla essence	Vanilla essence
Liquid sweetener	Liquid sweetener

1. Place dried skimmed milk in a 250ml (½-pint) mug; blend until smooth, with 2 x 15ml spoons (2 tablespoons) cold water.
2. Fill up mug with boiling water. Add vanilla essence and liquid sweetener to taste. Serve hot.
NOTE: Alternatively, make punch as above, but omit vanilla essence and add a few drops of raspberry-flavouring essence; colour with a few drops of pink food colouring, or use banana-flavouring essence and yellow food colouring.

Hot Tomato Cocktail *

(pictured on page 84)

For 2 portions:

IMPERIAL	METRIC
½ pint tomato juice	250ml tomato juice
½ level teaspoon meat extract	1 x 2.5ml spoons meat extract
Pepper	Pepper
Parsley	Parsley

1. Pour tomato juice into a measuring jug; make up to 375ml (¾ pint) with water.
2. Pour into a saucepan, stir in meat extract and bring to boil; season to taste with pepper. Pour into mugs and snip a little parsley over the surface. Serve hot, with celery, if desired.

Creamy Pea Soup *

(pictured on page 84)

For 2 portions:

IMPERIAL	METRIC
1 (5oz) can garden peas	1 (141g) can garden peas
2 rounded tablespoons dried skimmed milk	4 x 15ml spoons dried skimmed milk
1 chicken extract cube	1 chicken extract cube
½ teaspoon Worcestershire sauce	1 x 2.5ml spoons Worcestershire sauce
Pepper	Pepper

1. Press contents of can of peas through a sieve into a large saucepan. Mix together dried milk and 3 cans of water. Add to saucepan with chicken extract cube. Bring to boil, stirring continuously. Add Worcestershire sauce and season to taste with pepper. Serve hot.
NOTE: Alternatively, liquidise contents of can of peas, chicken extract cube, dried milk, and a can of water in an electric blender. Pour into saucepan and add 2 cans of water.

Hot Savoury Drink *

Makes 2 or 3 glasses:

IMPERIAL	METRIC
2 level teaspoons meat extract	1 x 10ml spoons meat extract
Boiling water	Boiling water
¼ pint tomato juice	125ml tomato juice
Salt and pepper	Salt and pepper

Place meat extract in a jug and add 250ml (½ pint) boiling water; stir until dissolved. Add tomato juice and a little salt and pepper. Mix well and pour into glasses.

Citrus Cup *

(pictured on page 84)

Makes 2 glasses:

2 medium-sized oranges
Half a lemon
Boiling water
Liquid sweetener (optional)

1. Scrub oranges and lemon. Using a sharp knife or potato peeler, pare rind from 1 orange and lemon, taking care not to include any white pith.
2. Place rind in a saucepan with about 125ml ($\frac{1}{4}$ pint) water. Bring to boil, cover and simmer for 5 minutes.
3. Cut 2 thin slices from centre of second orange and reserve for decoration. Squeeze juice from oranges and lemon; strain into a jug. Strain liquid from saucepan into jug, stir, then divide between 2 heatproof glasses.
4. Top up with boiling water and add liquid sweetener, if desired. Cut each reserved orange slice, from rind to centre and place one over the edge of each glass.

Orange and Lemon Drink *

Makes 1 glass:

IMPERIAL	METRIC
1 large orange	1 large orange
2 tablespoons lemon juice	2 x 15ml spoons lemon juice
Water or soda water	Water or soda water

1. Cut orange in half and cut off one thin slice from centre of orange. Squeeze juice from remainder of orange.
2. Place juice in a glass with lemon juice, and top up with water or soda water. Decorate with orange.

Jamaican Fizz *

Makes 2 glasses:

IMPERIAL	METRIC
1 medium-sized orange	1 medium-sized orange
A few drops rum essence	A few drops rum essence
2 (8.5 fluid oz) bottles low-calorie American dry ginger ale	2 (241ml) bottles low-calorie American dry ginger ale

1. Squeeze juice from orange and divide between 2 glasses. Add a few drops of rum essence to each glass.
2. Top up glasses with ginger ale, and serve immediately.

Frappé *

Makes 1 glass:

IMPERIAL	METRIC
1 heaped teaspoon instant coffee	3 x 5ml spoons instant coffee
3 or 4 ice cubes	3 or 4 ice cubes
Liquid sweetener	Liquid sweetener

1. Place instant coffee and ice cubes in a large plastic beaker with an air-tight lid. Add 250ml ($\frac{1}{2}$ pint) water and 3 or 4 drops of liquid sweetener.
2. Place lid firmly on beaker and shake contents well for about 1 minute, until a creamy foam forms on top. Pour into a tall glass; serve immediately.
NOTE: If not on a reducing diet, a small cube of ice cream can be added to glass.

Fresh Lemonade *

Makes 3 or 4 glasses:

IMPERIAL	METRIC
2 medium-sized lemons	2 medium-sized lemons
1 pint boiling water	500ml boiling water
Liquid sweetener	Liquid sweetener
Ice cubes	Ice cubes

1. Scrub lemons. Using a sharp knife or potato peeler, pare rind from lemons, taking care not to include any white pith. Place in a measuring jug. Add boiling water; leave until cold, then strain.
2. Squeeze juice from lemons; place in jug. Sweeten to taste with liquid sweetener.
3. Place ice cubes in glasses and pour on lemonade.

Lime Tea Punch *

(pictured on page 76)

Makes 8 to 12 glasses:

IMPERIAL	METRIC
$\frac{1}{2}$ pint undiluted low-calorie lime drink	250ml undiluted low-calorie lime drink
3 rounded teaspoons instant tea	2 x 15ml spoons instant tea
$\frac{1}{4}$ pint boiling water	125ml boiling water
3 (8.5 fluid oz) bottles low-calorie American dry ginger ale	3 (241ml) bottles low-calorie American dry ginger ale
1 tray ice cubes	1 tray ice cubes
Lemon slices	Lemon slices

1. Place lime drink and 750ml ($1\frac{1}{2}$ pints) cold water in a large serving jug. Dissolve instant tea in 125ml ($\frac{1}{4}$ pint) boiling water in a basin and add to jug; chill thoroughly.
2. Just before serving, add ginger ale, ice cubes and lemon slices.

Reading from left are:
ORANGE ICE CREAM SODA
ORANGE AND LEMON
FIZZ, ICED COFFEE, ORANGE
COCKTAIL, STRAWBERRY
MILKSHAKE, PINEAPPLE
PUNCH, LIME 'N'
GINGER COOLER ICED TEA

Orange Ice Cream Soda

Makes 1 glass:

IMPERIAL	METRIC
2 tablespoons undiluted low-calorie orange drink	2 x 15ml spoons undiluted low-calorie orange drink
1 small cube vanilla ice cream	1 small cube vanilla ice cream
Soda water	Soda water
Slice of orange	Slice of orange

Place orange drink in a large glass. Add ice cream; top up with soda water. Decorate with orange.

Orange and Lemon Fizz ✻

Makes 1 glass:

IMPERIAL	METRIC
2 tablespoons undiluted low-calorie lemon drink	2 x 15ml spoons undiluted low-calorie lemon drink
1 (8.5 fluid oz) bottle low-calorie sparkling orange	1 (241ml) bottle low-calorie sparkling orange
Ice cubes	Ice cubes
Twist of orange peel	Twist of orange peel
Slice of lemon	Slice of lemon

Place lemon drink in a glass; add sparkling orange and ice cubes. Arrange orange peel and quartered lemon slice on a cocktail stick; place stick across top of glass.

Iced Coffee *

Makes 1 glass:

IMPERIAL	METRIC
2 rounded teaspoons instant coffee (or to taste)	2 x 10ml spoons instant coffee (or to taste)
$\frac{1}{4}$ pint boiling water	150ml boiling water
Ice cubes	Ice cubes
2 rounded tablespoons dried skimmed milk	4 x 15ml spoons dried skimmed milk
Liquid sweetener	Liquid sweetener

1. Place instant coffee in a tall glass. Place a spoon in glass and pour on boiling water; stir, until coffee has dissolved. Stir in 1 ice cube and skimmed milk.
2. Top up glass with remaining ice cubes; stir well. Sweeten to taste with liquid sweetener.

Orange Cocktail *

Makes 1 glass:

IMPERIAL	METRIC
3 shakes aromatic bitters	3 shakes aromatic bitters
1 tablespoon undiluted low-calorie orange drink	1 x 15ml spoon undiluted low-calorie orange drink
$\frac{1}{4}$ pint soda water or low-calorie tonic water	150ml soda water or low-calorie tonic water
Ice cubes	Ice cubes

Place bitters and orange drink in glass. Top up with soda water or tonic water and ice cubes.

Strawberry Milkshake *

(pictured on pages 88, 89)

Makes 1 glass:

IMPERIAL	METRIC
3oz fresh or frozen strawberries	75g fresh or frozen strawberries
3 to 4 ice cubes, crushed	3 to 4 ice cubes, crushed
2 level tablespoons dried skimmed milk	2 x 15ml spoons dried skimmed milk
Liquid sweetener (equal to 3 teaspoons sugar)	Liquid sweetener (equal to 1 x 15ml spoon sugar)

1. Wash strawberries. Reserve one for decoration; hull remainder. Place in goblet of liquidiser. Add 150ml ($\frac{1}{4}$ pint) water and run machine until strawberries are broken down.

2. Add ice cubes, milk and liquid sweetener. Run machine for 1 minute. Pour into a glass and press reserved strawberry on to edge of glass. Serve immediately.

NOTE: If using frozen strawberries, omit ice cubes, if desired.

Iced Tea *

(pictured on page 89)

Makes 1 glass:

IMPERIAL	METRIC
Ice cubes	Ice cubes
2 teaspoons lemon juice	2 x 5ml spoons lemon juice
Strong hot tea	Strong hot tea
Slice of lemon	Slice of lemon
Sprig of mint (optional)	Sprig of mint (optional)
Liquid sweetener (optional)	Liquid sweetener (optional)

Fill a tall glass with ice cubes. Add lemon juice; strain on tea. Place a slice of lemon on edge of glass; add mint and liquid sweetener, if desired.

Dry White Wine Cup

Makes 8 to 10 glasses:

IMPERIAL	METRIC
1 bottle dry white wine	1 bottle dry white wine
8 tablespoons undiluted low-calorie lemon drink	8 x 15ml spoons undiluted low-calorie lemon drink
1 pint soda water	$\frac{1}{2}$ litre soda water
Ice cubes	Ice cubes
A few raspberries	A few raspberries

Place wine and lemon drink in a jug. Just before serving, add soda water, ice cubes and raspberries.

Lime 'n' Ginger Cooler *

(pictured on page 89)

Makes 1 glass:

IMPERIAL	METRIC
1 tablespoon low-calorie lime drink	1 x 15ml spoon low-calorie lime drink
1 (8.5 fluid oz) bottle low-calorie American dry ginger ale	1 (241ml) bottle low-calorie American dry ginger ale
Slices of lime or a sprig of mint	Slices of lime or a sprig of mint

Place lime drink in a glass; top up with ginger ale. Decorate with slices of lime or a sprig of mint.

NOTE: If not on a reducing diet, a tablespoon of gin may be added, if desired.

Pineapple Punch

(pictured on page 89)

Makes 8 to 10 glasses:

IMPERIAL	METRIC
1 pint unsweetened pineapple juice	500ml unsweetened pineapple juice
2 to 3 tablespoons dark rum	2 to 3 x 15ml spoons dark rum
Ice cubes	Ice cubes
2 (8.5 fluid oz) bottles low-calorie sparkling orange	2 (241ml) bottles low-calorie sparkling orange
Orange slices	Orange slices
Fresh raspberries	Fresh raspberries
Sprigs of mint (optional)	Sprigs of mint (optional)

Place pineapple juice, rum and ice cubes in a jug. Add sparkling orange, orange slices, raspberries and sprigs of mint, if desired.

St. Clement's Cup *

Makes 6 to 8 glasses:

IMPERIAL	METRIC
$\frac{1}{4}$ pint undiluted low-calorie lemon drink	150ml undiluted low-calorie lemon drink
$\frac{1}{4}$ pint undiluted low-calorie orange drink	150ml undiluted low-calorie orange drink
$\frac{1}{4}$ pint cold tea	150ml cold tea
Ice cubes	Ice cubes
$1\frac{1}{4}$ pints soda water	750ml soda water
Slices of orange (optional)	Slices of orange (optional)

Place lemon drink, orange drink and cold tea in a jug. Add ice cubes; top up with soda water. Float orange slices on top, if desired.

Exercise is a must, if you want a firm, trim figure. Go gently at first, if you're not in the habit of exercising and especially if some of the exercises seem a little difficult. Exercises should be fun to do, not tiring, and well within your own capabilities. When you finish exercising, you should have a feeling of achievement – that's why it's best to tailor each exercise to your ability, by doing as many as you feel you can manage, plus one. Incorporate as many as you can into your daily routine.

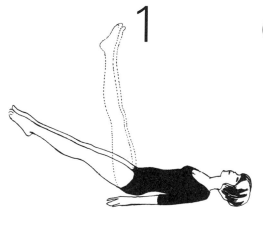

EXERCISES TO TONE AND TRIM

TUMMY:
1. Lie flat on your back, raise legs, so they are at right angles to the floor, then slowly lower them, both together, keeping knees stiff.
2. Lie flat on your back, feet tucked under a chest or heavy chair. Clasp hands behind your head and slowly lift your body to a sitting position, breathing in as you rise. Slowly return to lying position, breathing out.
3. Kneel down with knees slightly apart. Bend backwards and touch both feet with your hands. Hold this position and count to ten, then come back to the first position and relax.

BUST:
4. Stand straight, feet together, arms behind back, wrists grasped loosely. Bend forward slowly; at the same time, raise arms high behind you.
5. Do this either sitting or standing. Grasp left wrist from above with right hand and the right wrist from below with left hand. Give a sharp push towards elbows with both hands: you will feel a distinct jerk as you do so.

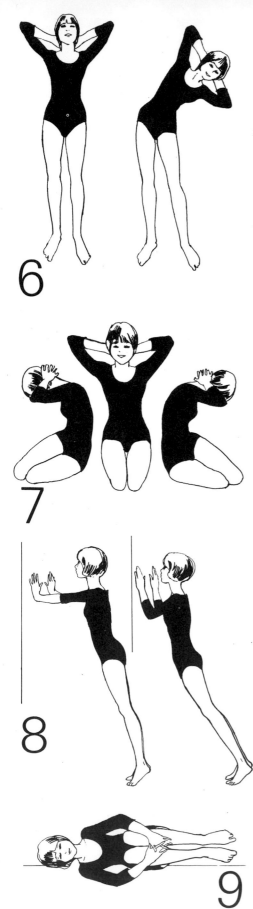

MIDRIFF AND WAIST:

6. Stand up, feet slightly apart. Clasp hands behind neck, pointing elbows upwards. Without moving feet, bend sideways to left, straighten up, then bend over to right, straighten again.

7. Kneel down, hands clasped behind neck. Keeping knees together, bend forward, pulling head downwards, and sit down of left side of your feet. Come back to original position again, then sit down to the right of your feet.

UPPER ARMS:

8. Stand facing a wall about a metre (1 yard) away, feet a little apart. Without moving feet, stretch arms straight out in front of you and move body forward until palms of hands are flat against wall at about shoulder level. Push hard against wall, then allow arms to bend, so palms and forearms are flat against wall. Press hard again; pull back to original position.

HIPS:

9. Lie on your back, with knees to chest, then roll right over, from one side to the other.

10. Lie face down on the floor, with a cushion under your tummy, arms by your sides on the floor. Stretch legs and point toes. Keeping right leg straight, raise it slowly off the floor, reaching up as high as possible (see sketch A). Bring leg back to floor slowly, at the same time raising left leg. When you become stronger, you can vary the exercise by raising both legs together as high as you possibly can (see sketch B), then lift your head and raise your arms, to rest by your thighs (C); then relax.

THIGHS:

11. Lie on your side, supporting yourself on elbow and lower arm. Raise both legs about 22cm (9in) off floor, keeping knees straight. Hold position for five seconds, lower legs slowly and relax.

12. Stand erect, one hand resting on edge of a heavy table or window ledge. Rise on tip-toe (keep back straight), bend knees slightly and bounce down, stopping when bottom is about 30cm (12in) above backs of ankles. Hold position for a moment before slowly rising to standing position.

BOTTOM:

13. Walk across floor on buttocks, with hands stretched ahead, eight paces forward, eight paces back, keeping the back as straight as possible.

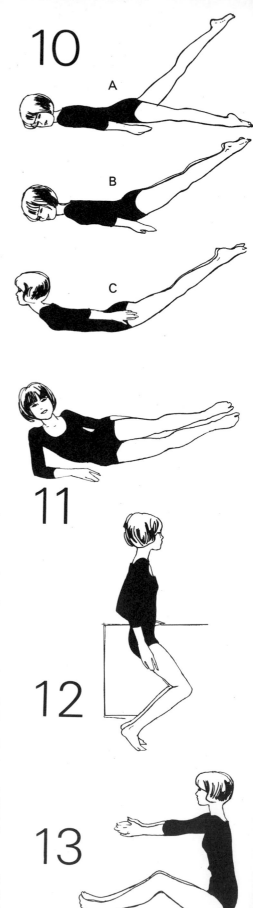

INDEX

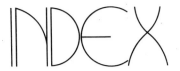

INDEX

First published in 1974 by FAMILY CIRCLE, Elm House, Elm Street, London, WC1X 0BP.
Third reprint 1978. Typeset by Apex Typesetting Ltd. Printed in England by Sackville Press Billericay Ltd.
1974 © Standbrook Publications Ltd., a Member of The Thompson Organisation Ltd.
Distributed to the book trade by Elm Tree Books/Hamish Hamilton Ltd.
Garden House 57/59 Long Acre London WC2E 9JZ
ISBN 0 241 10289 8